Silent and Undecided Friends

Motivating Greater LGBT Rights Advocacy Among Clergy and Congregations

Steve Clapp

A LifeQuest Publication

Silent and Undecided Friends

Silent and Undecided Friends:
Motivating Greater LGBT Rights Advocacy Among Clergy and Congregations

By Steve Clapp

Copyright © 2007, 2008 by LifeQuest, an imprint of Christian Community, Inc. Permission is extended to LGBT rights organizations, to clergy, and to other religious leaders working for justice to duplicate information from this report for use within denominations, congregations, state organizations, or other settings where the information will be of assistance. We ask only that copyright acknowledgment be given to Christian Community for the information. This report may not be duplicated in whole or in part for commercial purposes or for sale without written permission.

For further information, contact: LifeQuest, 6404 S. Calhoun Street, Fort Wayne, Indiana 46807; DadofTia@aol.com; (260) 456–5010. LifeQuest is a publishing imprint of Christian Community, Inc. www.churchstuff.com

Biblical quotations, unless otherwise noted, are from the New Revised Standard Version of the Bible, copyrighted 1989 by the Division of Christian Education, National Council of Churches and are used by permission.

The research and development on which this booklet is based were funded by a private family foundation, by the Arcus Gay and Lesbian Fund, and by Christian Community, Inc. The research was done independently of any denominational advocacy group.

ISBN 10: 1-893270-45-9
ISBN 13: 978-1-893270-45-9

Library of Congress Control Number: 2008925263

Manufactured in the United States

*"'You shall love the Lord your God
with all your heart, and with all your soul,
and with all your strength, and with all your mind;
and your neighbor as yourself.'"*
Luke 10:27 [NRSV]

*"Silence in the face of evil is itself evil;
God will not hold us guiltless.
Not to speak is to speak. Not to act is to act."*
Dietrich Bonhoeffer

*"'Don't be bluffed into silence by the threat of bullies.
There's nothing they can do to your soul, your core being.
Save your fear for God, who holds your entire life—
body and soul—in his hands.'"*
Matthew 10:28 [The Message]

Silent and Undecided Friends

Contents

An Inadequate Word	5
Executive Summary	7
Grandson Trumps Theology	14
Congregational Health	17
The LGBT Rights Project	19
Fine Print	23
Black Swans	26
Orientation and Science	28
The Information Gap	32
Homosexuality and Scripture	34
Congregational Acceptance	42
Concerns about Youth	47
Welcoming and Affirming Organizations	55
Integration into Broader Studies	69
Affirmation of Civil Rights	72
Licensing and Ordination	76
The Need for LGBT People in Congregations	78
Definitions	85
Organizations You May Wish to Know About	89
Resources from Christian Community	95

An Inadequate Word

THANKS is often an inadequate word when the contributions of so many people have been so crucial to a project and a publication. This report is part of a larger project called *LGBT Rights: Strategies for People of Faith*. The following have all made extremely important contributions to the project and this report:

- The Arcus Gay and Lesbian Fund which provided the primary support for the surveys, interviews, focus groups, and work with pilot congregations that have made this report and the broader *LGBT Rights: Strategies for People of Faith* project possible.

- Urvashi Vaid and Tom Kam, whose encouragement and counsel continue to help Christian Community build relationships with others working for justice. Linda May has also given us significant guidance in our work.

- The commitment of the Christian Community Board of Directors in moving beyond the relatively safe development areas of stewardship, church growth, worship, and Christian education into the area of religion and sexuality.

- The 1,511 clergy and other religious leaders who responded to our written surveys and the 268 who participated in phone interviews.

- The 105 people who participated in focus groups at various stages in the project leading to this report, and the 61 congregations that piloted activities as part of the overall project.

- My colleagues Jan Fairchild, Debra Haffner, Kristen Leverton Helbert, Aida Orgocka, Stacey Sellers, Holly Sprunger, Dan Wallace, Roberta Walters, and Angela Zizak who helped with various phases of this project.

Silent and Undecided Friends

I am humbled that so many people have contributed in so many ways to our work. My prayer is that this report and the related resources being developed as part of the *LGBT Rights: Strategies for People of Faith* project will enable fuller and more loving acceptance of LGBT persons in congregations, denominations, and society and a greater recognition of the spiritual gifts that LGBT persons bring.

                                              Steve Clapp
                                              President
                                              Christian Community, Inc.

Executive Summary

This report is based on surveys of 1,511 clergy from 32 different denominations; telephone interviews with 268 clergy; many focus group meetings; and work with 61 pilot congregations. The surveys, interviews, and focus groups were designed to gain:

- better understanding of effective practices to motivate clergy who feel positive toward LGBT people to take proactive actions on their behalf.

- better understanding of effective practices to move those who are undecided toward affirmation of LGBT people.

- better understanding of effective practices to use in congregations to gain greater acceptance of LGBT people and greater willingness to work for the rights of LGBT people.

Those strategies were tested in work with the 61 pilot congregations. This report is one of three publications growing out of the **LGBT Rights: Strategies for People of Faith** project. The other two publications are a booklet, *Taking a New Look: Why Congregations Need LGBT Members* and a larger publication, *LGBT Rights: A Strategy Manual for People of Faith*.

The clergy for this study were not randomly chosen but were selected because of the probability that they were silent or undecided friends of LGBT people. Some of the key findings of this project that are discussed in this report include:

- When pushed to choose between biology and environment as a primary source of sexual orientation, 66% of the clergy agreed that orientation is largely a matter of biology while 32% identified environment as the primary influence. Thirty-seven percent of the clergy responding believe that it is possible to change from a homosexual to a heterosexual orientation through therapy; those clergy have been heavily influenced by the work of organizations like Focus on the Family.

- We found a substantial number of clergy, in our phone interviews, who are warmly inclined on LGBT issues but who are lacking in factual knowledge and in strategies. Some of those who were interviewed are aware of the lack of knowledge, but they haven't taken the initiative to increase their understanding. Others have inaccurate information without being aware of it. Very few clergy, even in the more progressive denominations like the United Church of Christ, understand the concept of transgender. While we are disappointed in the amount of misinformation or lack of information that people have, this is an area that can be corrected.

- In the phone interviews, it became evident that many of the clergy who see the Old and/or New Testament Scriptures as clearly prohibiting homosexuality and as binding on behavior today are not open to alternative ways of interpreting those biblical passages. Efforts to explain the historical context of those passages do not appear to be successful in most instances. Sophisticated theological explanations about LGBT rights and the Bible are not understood or accepted by large numbers of clergy, which means that they are not likely to be effective with many people in the pews who are influenced strongly by those clergy.

The difficulty of getting clergy to see those passages differently than they have in the past does not mean that Scripture is without value in working toward a more accepting view of LGBT people. We find in fact that biblical accounts like the parable of the Good Samaritan [Luke 10:25–37] can be used to create a deeper concern about the rights of LGBT people regardless of their style of biblical interpretation. We also found in our work with pilot congregations that the biblical emphasis on hospitality has considerable power to motivate different attitudes and behaviors toward LGBT people. Passages like Genesis 18:1–15 and Hebrews 13:1–2 encourage showing hospitality to others, and those passages reflect the broad approach to hospitality that was taken in biblical times.

- We find a total of 71% of the respondents feeling that gay and lesbian persons can find welcome and acceptance in their congregation, but for some that welcome and acceptance are contingent on celibacy and in some instances even on working to change to a heterosexual orientation. **Only 41% of the respondents indicated an unqualified welcome.**

    Fifty-seven percent of the surveyed clergy *personally* agree or strongly agree that homosexual persons should be fully welcomed and accepted as members and participants in the life of the church without qualification. **The fact that 16% of the responding clergy personally support full acceptance without qualification but are in congregations that they do not perceive ready to grant that full acceptance suggests that there may be room for these clergy to have greater influence.**

    In addition to the 57% of clergy personally supporting welcome and acceptance without qualification, another 19% of the clergy support welcome and acceptance but qualify it with the desire for celibacy or for active work to change to a heterosexual orientation.

- Ministers who at first seem rather rigid in their disapproval of homosexual behavior begin to soften considerably when the subject of teens is raised with them. Christian Community has, from other research that we have done (published in the book *Faith Matters*), significant data about what gay, lesbian, and bisexual teens have experienced in congregational life, and we are finding that information very useful in talking with clergy.

    We found that almost all the congregations participating in the *Faith Matters* study had at least one teen who self-identified as gay, lesbian, bisexual, or questioning his or her orientation. **Eighty-six percent of those teens, however, said that their clergyperson was not aware of** their orientation or their struggle; 46% of them indicated that their parents did not know about their orientation or their struggle. When we surveyed the clergy in those congregations, only 18% thought that they had one or more LGBT teens in the congregation, and only 12% knew the name of a gay or lesbian teen.

Non-heterosexual teens in the *Faith Matters* study were almost twice as likely as heterosexual teens to have seriously considered suicide. This should be a matter of significant concern for those of us in faith-based institutions. And almost all the clergy with whom we visited in the interviews as part of the process leading to the report you are reading right now indicated that they are very concerned about this fact. There have been some recent secular studies indicating that non-heterosexual teens may not be as much at risk for suicide and depression as previously thought. We wonder if it is possible that the risk for religious teens is slightly higher because of the frequent conflict between their perceived orientation and the teachings of their congregation.

- Virtually all the clergy we surveyed in denominations that have welcoming and affirming groups were aware of the existence of the groups and of their mission. Because these groups are working for justice in their denominations and are in some instances pushing clergy and congregations to deal with LGBT concerns, it's not surprising that some clergy have strong feelings about the groups. There are clergy who are deeply supportive of their work, there are clergy who are opposed to their work, and there are also clergy who are made uncomfortable by their work.

    Fifty-two percent of the clergy were positive or at least neutral about the groups, but 48% expressed the opinion that the groups were currently doing more harm than good. That 48% were not necessarily opposed to greater LGBT welcome and acceptance in congregations. The phone interviews suggest to us that some clergy were simply reflecting their own lack of comfort dealing with LGBT concerns, and some were reflecting honest misgivings about the role of the group in their denomination.

Motivating Greater LGBT Rights Advocacy

The LGBT rights groups within denominations are perceived by some clergy as being managed and influenced primarily by gay and lesbian persons, who are perceived as having a personal "agenda." Several clergy indicated in phone interviews that these groups need more visible heterosexual allies, though not all who said that were willing to be those allies!

- There are many excellent studies on homosexuality that have been developed for use in congregations. There are also many excellent books that have been written on topics like homosexuality and the Bible. We need to be aware, however, that some clergy who are not yet ready to push a study focused primarily on homosexuality are open to the topic being covered in a broader study. Several of the pilot congregations with which we worked chose to integrate a study of homosexuality into a broader study of human rights, of religion and sexuality, or of hospitality. The quality of the discussions on homosexuality generated by those approaches was very high.

The sixteen congregations that used the hospitality framework for their study all generated statements out of the study process that supported a broad hospitality that included people of all sexual orientations. The biblical passages on hospitality offer little "wiggle room" for excluding certain categories of people, and church members identify positively with the images of themselves as hospitable people.

In our work with pilot congregations, we cooperated with several clergy on efforts to integrate LGBT concerns into sermons and worship in substantive ways that were comfortable for the minister and the congregation.

- Even clergy who are ambivalent about the involvement of homosexual persons within the life of the congregation reflect a commitment to the protection of the civil rights of homosexual persons. In fact the level of that commitment was much higher than we had anticipated prior to conducting the survey. Ninety-three percent support laws that protect the civil rights of homosexual persons; 62% support civil unions for homosexual persons; and 37% support the right to marry for homosexual persons.

- **Clergy who have been silent friends and clergy who remain undecided on LGBT issues are often almost painfully aware of the risks they take if they become openly supportive. There has been far too little focus on helping them recognize the cost of not being welcoming and accepting of LGBT people. Consider some of these costs that were identified in the study:**

    – The loss of involvement of LGBT persons, who are more numerous in society than most people realize.

    – The cost to families who have LGBT persons and feel unable to talk about that or to feel supported by the congregation.

    – The loss of involvement of young adults who have a different view of these issues than many older adults. With churches so often in desperate need of more young adults, this is a serious matter.

    – The perpetuation of a negative view of Christianity within the broader society, especially among young adults.

    – The loss of involvement of heterosexual people who find judgmental attitudes toward LGBT people unacceptable.

    – The loss of gifted LGBT clergy and other professional staff like music directors and business administrators who have much to offer the church.

    – The loss of the gifts of LGBT lay persons who have much to offer the church.

    – The feeling of LGBT people in the church that they must keep their orientation hidden.

- The cost to youth who are themselves LGBT or who are struggling over questions of orientation. Our congregational silence may well contribute to the increased suicide risk for religious LGBT teens.

- Inadequate sexuality education for children, teens, and adults because we are not willing to discuss issues of sexuality. This reality may contribute to higher rates of HIV and other sexually transmitted diseases, more unwanted pregnancies, and less satisfactory sexual relationships in marriages.

- A failure to show the kind of expansive hospitality that God expects.

- A failure to stand firmly for human rights and justice on this and other issues.

- The insights that we can gain from those who have been oppressed and the painful reality that, by our silence, we become part of the oppression.

- The personal distress and even damage to the soul caused by the disconnect some silent friends have between their personal convictions and their public vocalization.

For a fuller discussion of the gifts that LGBT involvement brings to congregations, see our booklet *Taking a New Look: Why Congregations Need LGBT Members*.

Grandson Trumps Theology

In our book ***Widening the Welcome of Your*** Church, my colleague Fred Bernhard and I share this account:

A prominent Mennonite church leader, whose name would be immediately recognized by many if we used it here, found his view of homosexuality challenged when his twenty-year-old grandson came out as gay. He described it in this way:

"I've always been pretty conservative on this issue. I recognize that the Bible doesn't say a great deal about homosexuality, but what is there has always seemed to me to be prohibitive. But now I find myself with a grandson, who never wanted to be gay, who has concluded that it is part of who he is, part of how God made him.

*"I held that little boy in my arms thirty minutes after his birth, and he has spent at least a week in my home every year of his life. I'm starting to take a new look at what the Bible says about sexuality, and I'm paying more attention to the Genesis story of creation, the context of the relatively small number of prohibitions, and the strong teachings of Christ about love. I haven't sorted it all out theologically, but I have to say this: **A grandson trumps theology**. You are looking at a new gay rights activist."*

The way that most of us feel about LGBT rights depends on a number of factors. Certainly those of us who are members of churches and other faith-based institutions are influenced by clergy, the Scriptures, official denominational positions, and what others in the congregation think and believe. We are also strongly influenced by our relationships, by compassion, and by love. Those, like the Mennonite leader, who have warm feelings for a friend or family member who comes out as gay, lesbian, bisexual, or transgender, may change the relative weight they give other factors.

The fact that you are reading these pages says that you are likely supportive of full rights for LGBT people and that you would like to see them fully included in congregational and denominational life. And like those responsible for this report, you are likely dismayed at the ways in which religious forces have worked against LGBT rights in the United States and have caused LGBT people to feel unwelcome in some congregational settings. The alliance of right-wing religious forces with right-wing political forces in the United States is especially disturbing and has done considerable harm to efforts to increase the rights of LGBT people.

You also know that clergy can play a very key role in determining the attitude of the congregation toward GLBT persons and toward the rights of those persons. While it is possible to take some initiatives for greater LGBT acceptance in a congregation in the presence of a negative or silent clergyperson, it's far easier to make a difference when clergy are openly supportive.

Virtually every denomination has some wonderful clergy who are **openly supportive** of the full acceptance of LGBT persons and who are activists on behalf of LGBT rights within the congregation, the denomination, and society.

There are also clergy who are **absolutely opposed** to LGBT rights and who exert considerable negative influence on people in their congregations and in the community. Some of the greatest opposition to LGBT rights in the United States has come from clergy and other religious leaders who have national prominence and frequent exposure in the media.

This report focuses primarily on clergy whom we describe as "silent and undecided friends" of LGBT people. There are many clergy who are **largely silent** in their congregations, their denominations, and public settings but who in fact are supportive of LGBT persons, want to see them fully accepted in congregations and in society, and want to see their rights protected and expanded. In private conversations with LGBT persons and heterosexual advocates, they will voice their support but will generally share reasons why the timing is not right for them to do more within their congregations or the public square. If those persons can be mobilized to do more on behalf of LGBT rights, they have the potential to influence large numbers of persons and to make a significant, positive difference.

Silent and Undecided Friends

There are also many clergy who are **undecided** on LGBT issues. They aren't hateful or negative toward LGBT people, and they are inclined toward warmth and acceptance. For a variety of reasons, they haven't arrived at or been willing to articulate a clear position. In some instances, they are uncomfortable about going in opposition to the prohibitive biblical passages or to the negative positions of denominational leaders. In some instances, they are so concerned about the potential for conflict within the congregation that they haven't pushed themselves to think through the love and justice issues involved. There are some of these clergy who simply feel too overwhelmed by the range of needs in their congregations and in society to have focused much intellectual or spiritual energy on LGBT concerns. Yet these clergy, the authors of this report are convinced, need to be viewed as friends of LGBT people. They are not negative, they are not hostile, they are inclined toward acceptance, and it should be possible to change their "undecided" positions.

And of course there are lay persons who reflect similar positions on LGBT matters. If silent and undecided clergy can be convinced to become allies with LGBT people and to actively work for acceptance, they can influence the very large numbers of silent and undecided lay persons in their congregations and in their communities.

The focus of this report is on better understanding where clergy are at on these issues and on identifying strategies which can be useful in making allies of those who have been largely silent or undecided on LGBT issues.

Congregational Health

This report grows out of work conducted by Christian Community, Inc. Christian Community is a nonprofit religious research and program development organization. Our organizational mission is to improve the health of congregations and of the communities in which congregations minister. Knowing a little more about the scope of our work may be helpful to you as you read this report.

We are not a secular organization, and we are not a LGBT denominational advocacy group. Our staff and board include persons across the spectrum of sexual orientation. While our name obviously indicates a Christian orientation, we work cooperatively with persons of the Jewish, Islamic, Hindu, and Buddhist traditions in the process of doing some of our practical research projects. When seeking ways to improve the health of communities in which congregations minister, we are also pleased to work with people who do not profess any religious faith but who share our concerns for the poor, for justice, and for peace.

Much of our work in the past has focused on such traditional areas of congregational health as stewardship, hospitality, church growth, worship, Christian education, and helping congregations become more multicultural. Over 18,000 congregations have cooperated with us on research projects and utilized resources that we've developed. Readers of this report may be familiar with our hospitality resources, including **Widening the Welcome of Your Church** and with our stewardship resources like **Cell Phones, Dessert, and Faith**.

In the process of doing congregational studies, the Christian Community staff and board became increasingly aware of the extent to which most congregations seemed to be doing very little to help people relate their faith to their sexuality.

We were disturbed that so many churches were doing nothing to help their teenagers prepare for sexual decision-making, dating,

Silent and Undecided Friends

marriage, or parenting. We found many congregations that have stated positions against premarital intercourse but who in fact have large numbers of young adults who are living together and who are not married. And divorce rates in virtually all congregations, whether liberal or conservative, have continued to be high, suggesting that we have not learned how to help couples communicate well about sexuality and many other topics. We also became concerned, as we worked with congregations in the area of hospitality, that so many were hostile toward LGBT persons or simply wanted to avoid having anything to do with LGBT issues.

Congregations that are not helping people relate their faith to their sexuality and that are avoiding dealing with so many issues are not as healthy as they should be. Christian Community determined that work at the intersection of religion and sexuality would become a major area of focus for us in new program development.

Our first major project on religion and sexuality was a study on how the religious beliefs and congregational activity of teenagers related to their sexual values and behaviors. The results of that study were published in the book **Faith Matters: Teenagers, Religion, and Sexuality** and also provided the basis for our book **The Gift of Sexuality: Empowerment for Religious Teens** and the accompanying **Adult Guide** to that publication.

We also have the privilege of working with the Religious Institute on Sexual Morality, Justice, and Healing, which was started by Debra Haffner and has become an important part of the work of Christian Community. That organization focuses on justice, morality, and healing in creative and effective ways. The Religious Institute publication **A Time to Seek: Study Guide on Sexual and Gender Diversity** by Tim Palmer and Debra Haffner is an outstanding resource for those wanting to better understand the factual background on these concerns. The Institute also developed **An Open Letter to Religious Leaders on Sexual and Gender Diversity** with the involvement of several prominent theologians.

The full acceptance of LGBT people in congregations, denominations, and society has been of great concern to us for many years. Most of the congregations that have worked with us on research projects and on resource development and that have used our resources are mainline or evangelical Protestant. Because of our existing relationships with those congregations, we increasingly began to realize that we were well positioned to start having more influence on LGBT matters. That realization marked the beginning of the project described in the next section.

The LGBT Rights Project

We've carried out practical research to find the most effective ways to enable congregations to change in how they handled areas like stewardship, hospitality, church growth, and multicultural outreach. We wanted to approach the area of LGBT rights in the kind of way we have found effective in working for change in other areas of the life of the church. As a result, we started the *LGBT Rights: Strategies for People of Faith* project with an initial emphasis on gathering information. That included these steps:

- Studying print and web resources to learn what others have been doing to work for greater acceptance and justice for LGBT people.

- We also studied the tactics and resources being used by those opposed to LGBT rights. We sought to better understand why some of those individuals and organizations have had so much impact.

- Visiting with theologians, denominational leaders, and others with insights on LGBT rights and the Christian faith.

- Conducting six focus groups to help us better identify the kinds of questions that we should ask and the kinds of information we needed to seek.

- Surveying 1,511 clergy and other religious leaders whom we believed likely to be progressive, moderate, or open on LGBT rights. While we intentionally wanted to reach some persons who were progressive, we especially hoped to reach those who were moderate or open. We surveyed people from 32 denominations. We wanted to understand how they felt about LGBT issues, why they felt that way, what the attitudes and practices were in their churches, and what approaches might be helpful in bringing about change for those persons who were undecided on LGBT issues.

- Interviewing 268 persons from 21 denominations who had completed written surveys for us to explore more fully what strategies would be effective in helping them work for greater LGBT acceptance and for support of LGBT rights within their congregations. We wanted to know both what had already proven effective for those clergy who had taken initiatives in their congregations and what strategies seemed most attractive and realistic for those who had not yet done anything significant in their congregations.

- Conducting focus groups again to identify the very best strategies for work with congregations.

- Working with clergy and other leaders in 61 congregations to pilot strategies to bring about greater acceptance of LGBT people in the congregation and greater willingness of people to work for LGBT rights in the congregation, the denomination, and society. The results of the work with those congregations are more fully shared in our publication **LGBT Rights: A Strategy Manual for People of Faith** than in the briefer report that you are currently reading.

Because the information shared in this report and the recommendations made are a direct outgrowth of the work just described, it's especially important for you to realize that this was not a random study. We worked with lists of clergy that we already had as a result of the other work of Christian Community. We selected from those lists clergy who seemed to us most likely to be progressive, moderate, or undecided on LGBT rights. We based those selections on factors like their denominational affiliation, the projects with which they had cooperated with us, the resources they had purchased from us, and the publications to which they subscribed.

We were not attempting to reach clergy who are actively opposed to LGBT rights. While we recognize the need to find ways to change the opinions of the opposition, that was not our focus in this project. We wanted to find clergy who were progressive because we could learn from those who were already doing a lot on behalf of LGBT rights and because we wanted to learn what would cause those who were not taking initiatives to be more willing to do so. We wanted to find clergy who were moderate because we wanted to understand what strategies or resources might cause them to become more progressive on LGBT rights and what strategies they felt would work in their congregations. And we wanted to find clergy who were undecided so that we could come to understand their indecision and the factors that would enable change for them and for their congregations.

We worked at this task with lists of those with whom we already had a relationship both because we had more existing data about those clergy to help in the selection process and because we felt that they would be more likely to cooperate with us by completing surveys and taking part in interviews. We used the description "clergy and other religious leaders" because we had responses from 53 persons who were Christian educators, youth workers, or seminary faculty involved in the life of a local congregation. All others were clergy.

We wanted to be sure that our surveys included good representation from the largest of the mainline Protestant denominations: the United Methodist Church, the Presbyterian Church USA, the American Baptist Churches, the United Church of Christ, the Evangelical Lutheran Church, the Episcopal Church, and the Disciples of Christ. While we were not looking primarily at Roman Catholic clergy, we did want to include some priests in our sample because of our desire to better understand the dynamics in the Roman Catholic Church. We also wanted to be sure that clergy from some predominantly African American denominations were part of the survey. We included persons from a few more conservative denominations because we felt that pastors from those denominations who were connected with Christian Community might be more progressive than others in their tradition on these issues and would have perspectives that would be valuable to us.

When we started the project, we were thinking of obtaining returned surveys from perhaps 200 to 300 people. As we began moving into the project, however, we decided that it was important

Silent and Undecided Friends

to increase the numbers significantly. While this is very much a non-random sample, having responses from 1,000 or more increases the usefulness and worth of the information obtained. We sent surveys to 3,720 clergy and other religious leaders and were delighted to receive 1,511 responses for a response rate of 40.6%.

Here are the numbers of congregations, by denomination, represented by clergy and other religious leaders who completed written surveys:

United Methodist Church	103
Presbyterian Church, USA	91
American Baptist Churches	87
United Church of Christ	86
Evangelical Lutheran Church	74
Episcopal Church	72
African Methodist Episcopal	70
Roman Catholic Church	64
Disciples of Christ	62
Church of the Brethren	52
African Methodist Episcopal Zion	52
Reformed Church in America	49
Assemblies of God	48
Church of God	47
Nazarene Church	45
Black Baptist Church	44
Christian Methodist Episcopal	42
Missouri Synod Lutheran Church	39
Mennonite Church	38
Progressive Baptist Church	36
Moravian Church	35
Evangelical Covenant Church	35
Independent Baptist Church	32
Friends/Quakers	29
Independent Christian Churches	29
Pentecostal Church	28
Cumberland Presbyterian Church	27
Church of Jesus Christ of Latter Day Saints	27
Unitarian Universalist	23
Brethren in Christ Church	19
Free Methodist Church	14

Missionary Church	12
Total	1,511

Fine Print

In *The Invisible Touch*, Harry Beckwith reminds us that "research changes its own results" [p. 7]. No matter how large the sample or how meticulous the research, there are many variables that cannot be controlled; and the research instruments and methods influence the results—sometimes in unanticipated ways. This section is the **fine print** about this report, suggesting the qualifications that you should keep in mind as you read it:

1. The fact that Christian Community had a previous relationship with virtually all of the survey respondents caused them, we think, to be more willing to complete the surveys and to be more candid with us. That same relationship, however, could also have caused them, in perhaps unconscious ways, to respond in the way that they think we "wanted" them to respond.

The letters that were sent with the written surveys were worded in a relatively neutral way and did not convey that we had as an organization already arrived at a position supportive of LGBT rights. We received phone calls both from persons wanting to know if we were against LGBT rights and from persons wanting to know if we were for LGBT rights in response to the letters and surveys being mailed.

People who had used our resources on youth and sexuality, however, would clearly have known from those resources that Christian Community is supportive of LGBT rights. Thus we have to assume that this fact had an impact on whether or not persons decided to return a survey and also on how they may have responded to the questions on the survey. This reality did not unduly concern us because we were not seeking responses from people actively opposed to LGBT rights, but it's important to be aware of the fact that the relationship of respondents to the organization could have biased some of their responses, perhaps in ways we do not recognize.

2. To repeat the caution shared in the previous section describing the project, this was not a random sample. Had we taken lists of all the clergy in the denominations and then selected every *nth* name to receive a survey, we would have been closer to a random sample. These clergy already had a relationship with us. That previous relationship might have been as minimal as their having ordered a single book or report from us or it might have been as significant as a clergyperson's church having participated with us in a major research project. Remember that we were not seeking to do a random study. We wanted to connect with clergy who would respond to us and who would be as candid as possible in expressing their opinions on the written surveys and in the follow-up phone interviews. We had considered the possibility of doing this as a more random study, but we rejected that because we felt the candor of responses was so important.

You may wish to be aware, however, that the majority of the names on the Christian Community lists have come from mailings that were sent to all of the clergy in several denominations. Thus those who have chosen to work with us on past projects or who have chosen to use our resources are the ones out of a particular denomination who were drawn to the kind of work we do.

3. It is important to remember that some of the data shared in this report results from bivariate analysis or cross-tabulation of the variables studied. The information provided is by association but is not necessarily causal. For those not familiar with statistical methodology, a classic analogy is that the population of storks in a given geographical area may increase at the same time as the birth rate increases for that area—but this does not prove that storks bring babies.

The written surveys indicate, for example, that clergy who both have one or more close friends who are gay or lesbian and also have one or more family members who are gay or lesbian are considerably more likely to have taken initiatives on behalf of gay rights in the congregation and in the community. This conclusion is logical and seems supportive of what common sense also suggests about the impact of relationships on how people feel about LGBT rights. But bivariate analysis does not prove a causal relationship.

Motivating Greater LGBT Rights Advocacy

4. We gave respondents to the written survey the option of not putting their names on the form, but we also asked them to indicate whether or not they were open to being contacted for a telephone interview. The majority did choose to put their name on the form and were open to a telephone interview. Had the form not given a place for the respondent's name and had a telephone interview as follow-up not been raised as a possibility, responses to the written survey might have been different.

5. An increasing number of persons speak not just of LGBT concerns but of LGBTQQI: gay, lesbian, bisexual, transgender, queer, questioning, and intersexual. Our written survey did not begin to go that far. The items included in our written survey were focused on the G and the L of LGBT concerns.

Bisexuality and transgender concerns were discussed in some telephone interviews but were not directly covered in the written surveys (aside from a few items about sexual orientation). QQI concerns only occasionally came up in the telephone inter-views.

We made a choice to focus on gay and lesbian concerns because of the high visibility of that issue in the life of the church today. The focus groups with which we met to help us in the design of the survey and interview instruments made it clear that very few congregations were dealing at all with the topics of bisexuality or transgender, let alone the broader queer, questioning, and intersexual designations. We came away from the focus groups feeling that an effort to cover BTQQI in the written survey would require our providing many definitions, would confuse some respondents, and would likely lower our response rate. In hindsight, we are not entirely convinced that was the right decision; but you need to know it was the decision that we made.

Thus the focus of this report on the whole is on homosexuality, though we do share perspectives on bisexuality and transgender concerns as those were raised in the telephone interviews. Please know that Christian Community organizationally is committed to the acceptance and the rights of all people of all sexual orientations and gender identities. We simply made pragmatic decisions on limiting the scope of the written survey based on the feedback of the focus groups.

Silent and Undecided Friends

Black Swans

Black Swan events are another factor of importance when looking at the positions of people on LGBT issues in the church. A Black Swan event is something that was not expected, that has a very significant impact, and that can be either positive or negative in nature. As shared earlier in this report, there are many different factors that impact how people of faith feel about homosexuality. Written surveys, by their nature, will only elicit the specific information and opinions requested. Telephone interviews have more latitude, and a skilled interviewer will explore conversational themes that may reveal information or motivation that would not otherwise have been identified.

The experience of the Mennonite leader described earlier in this report was a kind of Black Swan event in that person's life. It would not have been expected, and it obviously had profound impact on his beliefs and his practices. Had that person completed our written survey, he would no doubt have indicated having a family member who was homosexual; but he would likely not have written a lengthy comment that would have helped us understand the enormous impact of that event. A telephone interview with him would have been more likely to reveal the full impact of that event.

It is very important for us to learn all we can about the pragmatic steps that can be taken to build greater acceptance of LGBT persons in congregations and in society. We need to encourage clergy and congregations to take initiatives that will help bring about change using strategies that have proven successful in other settings. This report and our larger *Strategy Manual* are designed to help advocacy groups, clergy, and congregations develop such initiatives. At the same time, the biggest impact on an individual or a congregation may be something that was completely unanticipated:

- A loved family member comes out as gay.

- A couple gives birth to a child with atypical development of the external genitals, and the child cannot be readily said to be either male or female.

Motivating Greater LGBT Rights Advocacy

- A loved pastor comes out to the congregation as gay.

- A gay teen in the church attempts suicide.

- A well-known married couple has a divorce because one partner has determined that he or she is homosexual.

- A gay couple asks their pastor to perform a marriage service for them.

- A new member of the church is already deeply involved in an organization like Jerry Falwell Ministries or Focus on the Family, which has a strong anti-gay agenda.

- A new member of the congregation is already deeply involved in a LGBT advocacy group within the denomination.

All those events can have significant impact on how many people feel about LGBT issues. For the most part those are not events that can be predicted or controlled.

*If you want to learn more about the Black Swan phenomenon, see **The Black Swan** by Nassim Nicholas Taleb, a Random House publication, 2007.*

Orientation and Science

About two-thirds of the clergy we surveyed agree that sexual orientation is largely a matter of biology or involves a blend of biology and the environment, but a significant minority feels that a person with a homosexual orientation can change to a heterosexual orientation. (Here and in the sections that follow, the word "clergy" will be used to include both the 1,458 clergy and the 53 other religious leaders who completed written surveys.) Two statements in the survey pushed respondents to choose between biology or environment as a primary source of sexual orientation. Here are the percentages who strongly agreed or agreed with each of those statements:

66%   Sexual orientation (heterosexual, homosexual, bisexual) is largely a matter of biology.

32%   Sexual orientation is largely a matter of environmental influences.

In terms of strength of agreement, it's interesting to note that 40% *strongly* agreed that orientation is largely a matter of biology in contrast to only 6% who *strongly* agreed that orientation is largely a matter of environmental influences. Another item let people indicate that sexual orientation is a blend of biology and the environment, and over half agreed or strongly agreed with that statement:

58%   Sexual orientation involves a blend of biology and the environment.

Respondents were also given an opportunity to indicate whether or not it's possible to change sexual orientation:

37%   It is possible for a person who has a homosexual orientation to change to a heterosexual orientation.

As would be expected, most of those who felt that it was possible for a person of homosexual orientation to change to heterosexual orientation were persons who saw orientation being largely a matter of environmental influences, but 13% of those who saw orientation being largely a matter of biological influences nevertheless thought it was possible for orientation to be changed from homosexual to heterosexual. A significant minority of those who saw orientation being largely a matter of environmental influence did *not* think it was possible for orientation to be changed.

When one considers the fact that this sample of clergy consists primarily of those who are progressive, moderate, or at least open-minded on LGBT issues, it's of significant concern to find 37% thinking that a change of orientation is possible. In telephone interviews, persons holding the view that change is possible often cited the influence of organizations like Focus on the Family and others connected with what is often called the ex-gay movement.

The current ex-gay movement is thought by many to have begun in 1973 with the beginning of a group called "Love in Action" that focused on lesbians and gay men who wanted to change their orientation. That movement has continued, and Focus on the Family sponsors conferences and other events to give visibility to the ex-gay movement. Focus on the Family founder James Dobson believes that homosexuality can be prevented and that change of orientation is possible.

In understanding the impact of the ex-gay movement, it's important to recognize that there is what one of our telephone interviewers called a "slickness" to that movement with an effort to focus on compassion rather than on antagonism toward those of homosexual orientation and toward those protective of them. The ex-gay movement often says, for example, that people do not necessarily "choose" same-sex attraction but rather are conditioned for it by failures or perceptions of failure in early relationships. They also emphasize the importance of not blaming parents for the same-sex attraction of children. At the same time, they are firm in saying that family members should not be persuaded to accept homosexuality by the explanations of gay or lesbian family members. Leaders in the ex-gay movement speak compassionately about the uninformed opinions of those who oppose conversion therapy and do not recognize the power of prayer to change the lives of people.

To the knowledge of the author of this report, there are no peer-reviewed longitudinal studies on the success rate of conversion therapies (often called reparative therapies) of lesbian, gay, and bisexual people. A study reported by Robert Spitzer in the *Archives of Sexual Behavior* (October, 2003) suggests that people with high motivation can alter self-identity or sexual behavior but that it is almost impossible to reverse attraction to persons of the same sex. A Focus on the Family staff member interviewed by a Christian Community staff member made, on the condition of anonymity, this observation:

"It really doesn't matter whether or not the underlying attraction to the opposite sex can be changed. The ex-gay movement is about changing behavior, not attraction. Our point is that with good reparative therapy and the power of prayer, people can control their behavior and can begin to act in a heterosexual manner. The Spitzer report may be true, but that doesn't contradict our insistence that behavior can be controlled and that the Bible says it must be controlled."

It's easy to underestimate the influence of the ex-gay movement on the views of moderate and undecided clergy. They are inclined to put considerable weight on the statements of people in the ex-gay movement who claim to have changed from homosexual to heterosexual, and they are also impressed by the academic credentials of James Dobson and others in Focus on the Family. Most of the clergy who participated in telephone interviews and felt that orientation could be changed were completely unaware that the American Medical Association, the American Psychiatric Association, and other professional groups have take positions in opposition to conversion therapies. For example, in 2000, the American Psychiatric Association stated: "In the last four decades reparative therapists have not produced any rigorous scientific research to substantiate their claims of cure."

Sixty-six percent of these clergy agreed that orientation is largely a matter of biology. Even most of those who felt that it was largely a matter of environment agreed in phone interviews that people were not really "choosing" their sexual orientation. Here are some comments:

> *I used to think that people chose to be gay or lesbian, but that was before I knew any gay or lesbian people. Now it's clear to me that people aren't "deciding" to be gay. They just are gay. Biology has to have something to do with it; maybe the environment too.* United Methodist Minister

> *I know that they haven't found a gene that is specifically responsible for sexual orientation, but I think there is growing evidence that our DNA has something to do with the orientation that we have. I know we haven't done enough to help people in the church recognize this.* Missouri Synod Lutheran Minister

> *When I think of all the pain that some of the gay people I've known have gone through because of rejection by friends, family, and the church, I just have to think that they didn't "choose" to have this orientation. It's just a part of who they are, and that has to mean that it's part of God's plan.* Disciples of Christ Minister

It's also important to be aware that a person believing that it is possible to change from a homosexual orientation to a heterosexual orientation does not mean that such persons feel that kind of change *should* happen. In the telephone interviews, only three clergy who felt that change was possible actually shared the strong opinion that homosexual persons should be encouraged to change.

As most readers of this report are aware, we still do not fully understand the factors that cause a person to have a particular sexual orientation. What is clear is that most people don't consciously "choose" that they are going to be homosexual, heterosexual, or bisexual. The fact that significant numbers of clergy recognize that biological factors play a role in sexual orientation is encouraging. The fact that such a minority feels orientation can be changed says that considerable education needs to be done.

The Information Gap

We found a substantial number of clergy, in our phone interviews, who are warmly inclined on LGBT issues but who are lacking in factual knowledge and in strategies. Some of those who were interviewed are aware of the lack of knowledge, but they haven't taken the initiative to increase their understanding. Others have inaccurate information without being aware of it. Very few clergy, even in the more progressive denominations like the United Church of Christ, understand the concept of transgender. While we are disappointed in the amount of misinformation or lack of information that people have, this is an area that can be corrected. Consider some of these statements:

What is this business about people actually wanting to be called "queer"? I thought that was a horribly disrespectful thing to call someone, but I hear some young people calling themselves that. What's this about? African Methodist Episcopal Minister

Aren't bisexual people really people who are gay but just aren't ready to admit it? Evangelical Lutheran Minister

I just finished reading the book Middlesex. *I had thought that kind of condition, genital development that wasn't clearly male or female, was very, very rare. Then I found out a couple in my parish had a son with indeterminate genitalia but that the physician pushed them into early surgery to "create" a female. Why haven't we known more about this?* Roman Catholic Priest

I read Steve Clapp's book Faith Matters. *Before reading that, I had no idea that almost every church has teens who are gay or lesbian. We just all act like gays and lesbians are outside the church.* United Methodist Minister

This will probably sound incredibly ignorant to you, but I don't even understand how gay people have sex. Is one of the men always taking the part of a woman with the anus being the opening instead of the vagina? Or do they mainly give each

other oral sex? Or do they take turns? I do not know.
Progressive Baptist Minister

When I was growing up, my parents were worried about not doing something that would cause me to be a homosexual. They were concerned when I showed more interest in playing house than in playing baseball. And my father freaked once when I said that pink was my favorite color. . . . I turned out to be heterosexual, and I know that liking pink and wanting to play house didn't mean I was gay. But are there other things about how children are raised that can cause them to be heterosexual or homosexual? Disciples of Christ Minister

Is a person who wants to change from a male or a female (or vice versa) just by definition mentally ill? Can it possibly be "normal" to want to be something different than the way you were born? American Baptist Minister

The telephone interviews revealed many clergy needing more accurate information on a wide variety of topics. The lack of understanding of transgender was especially striking, and there was considerable confusion about the distinction between sexual orientation and gender. At the end of this report, we include some definitions from *A Time to Seek* that may be helpful to some readers.

The written surveys were primarily focused on gay and lesbian issues rather than topics like bisexuality, transgender, transsexuals, and intersexuals. On the basic of the focus groups we conducted prior to the development of the written survey, we determined to limit the focus of that survey to gay and lesbian issues. The telephone interviews endeavored to do more with the "B" and the "T" in LGBT. In our pilot work with congregations, we encouraged consideration of the full range of LGBT rights.

Homosexuality and Scripture

There is considerable variation in how these clergy view homosexuality in the Hebrew Bible or Old Testament and in the New Testament. The responses of some clergy from item to item concerned with the Scriptures appear less than consistent, which the phone interviews cause us to believe reflects, in part, the tension some clergy feel over the Scriptures and same sex relationships. It's also true that the Scriptures themselves contain some inconsistencies in their view of same sex relationships, with a small number of passages appearing prohibitive in nature and a large number of passages talking about the love and acceptance of God. Even intelligent, well-educated readers can be forgiven some uncertainty. We also need to keep in mind that the terms *heterosexual, homosexual, gay, lesbian,* and *bisexual* are modern terms–not biblical terms. Consider the percentage who agreed or strongly agreed with the following statements:

56% The Old Testament clearly prohibits homosexuality.

59% I do not think the Old Testament passages against homosexuality are binding on behavior today.

46% The New Testament clearly prohibits homosexuality.

55% When properly understood, the New Testament is not condemning homosexuality as we understand that orientation and behavior today.

51% The creation passages in Genesis about the goodness of creation support a positive view of homosexuality as a part of creation.

86% The parable of the Good Samaritan stands as a reminder that homosexual persons are our neighbors and should be treated with love and respect.

As many readers of this report are aware, there have been many efforts by scholars to provide a fuller context for the biblical passages that are normally cited in opposition to homosexuality, the passages that some refer to as the "clobber texts." For example:

Genesis 19:1–11 really is an account of abuse and assault rather than an attack on homosexuality.

Leviticus 18:22; Leviticus 20:13; and **Deuteronomy 23:17–18** are part of what was called the "purity code" in Old Testament times. That same code also prohibits sex with a woman who is menstruating. Other passages in these Old Testament books require styles of dress that we no longer follow. Parents are also told to stone disobedient children! We do not, fortunately, put equal weight on every instruction found in Leviticus and Deuteronomy. Thus we should not assume that the prohibition of same-sex behaviors given here should be applied to life today.

1 Corinthians 6:9 has an uncertain meaning, and it depends on the translation used. The New International Version translates a word as "homosexual" that the New Revised Standard Version translates as "male prostitutes."

Romans 1:26–27 seems one of the clearest New Testament prohibitions on same sex behavior. Some biblical scholars, however, have pointed out that Paul is not speaking here about those born with a homosexual orientation. He seems to be speaking about men who are heterosexual but who are having sex with other men—against their own orientation.

1 Timothy 1:10–11 may well have been condemning not homosexuality but pederasty, according to many biblical scholars. Pederasty was the practice of male teachers exploiting their position with male students by requiring them to have sexual relations with them. Thus these were not consensual acts and involved adults with children. In our own time, we would condemn such acts whether they were homosexual or heterosexual.

Silent and Undecided Friends

With all of the passages just identified, it's important to remember that life was very short in biblical times. People were married at a very young age and had as many children as possible. Mary may have been as young as fifteen or sixteen when she gave birth to Jesus. With many people not living far into their thirties, family size was very important. In that kind of culture, it's understandable that same sex behavior would have been discouraged.

The fact that it may have been discouraged does not necessarily mean that it is a sin. There are biblical passages that urge celibacy [not having sex at all], prohibit divorce, or expect women to be subservient to men. We do not consider those passages authoritative today. Why should we give strong weight to the very small number of passages that talk about homosexual behavior, especially given the context of those passages?

This seems especially true since Jesus doesn't mention same-sex behavior in the gospels at all. Jesus never felt a need to reference same-sex behavior or to prohibit it. If it were a sin, why is Jesus silent on the topic? There are some who maintain that in Matthew 19:11–12 Jesus is making a positive statement about sexual variation when he talks about eunuchs.

Many clergy feel that the Old Testament passages are not binding on people today and that the New Testament passages are not condemning homosexuality as we understand it today. Explanations like the ones just given are understood and accepted by most of those clergy.

In the phone interviews, it became evident that many of the clergy who see the Old and/or New Testament Scriptures as clearly prohibiting homosexuality and as binding on behavior today are not open to alternative ways of interpreting those biblical passages. Efforts to explain the historical context of those passages do not appear to be successful in most instances. Sophisticated theological explanations about LGBT rights and the Bible are not understood or accepted by large numbers of clergy, which means that they are not likely to be effective with many people in the pews who are influenced strongly by those clergy.

We are aware that many theologians and seminaries are convinced that a solution to the matter of biblical interpretation is how the minds of people will be changed on LGBT rights. **But our conversations leave us increasingly feeling that it is very difficult to win on the field of biblical interpretation.** It is almost impossible to change the position of moderates on these passages if they in fact are conservative in their biblical interpretation.

While we are certainly not opposed to (and in fact are highly supportive of) the efforts that some seminaries are making in this regard, we are increasingly convinced that changing the attitudes of the typical clergyperson and of persons in the congregation needs to be based on simpler arguments and an avoidance of debates about biblical interpretation. It is *very* difficult to convince someone with a seminary education that the way he or she has been interpreting the Bible is not correct.

Obviously, however, seminaries can play a very important role in shaping the attitudes and practices of those who are being trained for ministry. Our partner organization, The Religious Institute on Sexual Morality, Justice, and Healing is in the process of conducting an important study of how seminaries deal with issues of sexuality, including LGBT concerns.

Some readers of this report will be aware of the efforts made by liberal biblical scholars to show the Old Testament relationships of David and Jonathan and of Ruth and Naomi as possible examples of same-sex relationships being reported and respected in Scripture. David's words on hearing of the death of Jonathan in 2 Samuel 1:26 are especially compelling:

> *[G]reatly beloved were you to me;*
> *your love to me was wonderful,*
> *passing the love of women.*

Ruth had been married to the son of Naomi; but when both became widows, they forged a strong relationship with each other. These words of Ruth to Naomi in Ruth 1:16 have often been quoted and have even been used in heterosexual wedding services:

> *Where you go, I will go;*
> *Where you lodge, I will lodge;*
> *your people shall be my people,*
> *and your God my God.*

Our conversations with clergy, however, indicated that the stories of Ruth and Naomi and of Jonathan and David had very little motivating power for changing the perspective of moderate clergy. Even progressive clergy who personally found it possible that these are accounts of homosexual relationships said that the passages were not useful in persuading moderates or undecided people in their congregations. While we can infer a homosexual relationship between these couples, the passages are not clear about sexual intimacy. Ruth marries a man again; and while some refer to it as a marriage of economic necessity, others see it as confirmation of her fundamental heterosexuality. David had a rather active heterosexual lifestyle as is reflected in his love of Bathsheba, in his getting her pregnant, and in his willingness to send her husband into the thick of battle so that he would be killed and leave Bathsheba available. Indeed David had several wives and stands as an example of dismaying moral decisions.

The difficulty of getting clergy to see those passages differently than they have in the past does not mean that Scripture is without value in working toward a more accepting view of LGBT people. We find in fact that biblical accounts like the parable of the Good Samaritan [Luke 10:25–37] can be used to create a deeper concern about LGBT people regardless of biblical interpretation.

A Samaritan man is the hero of that parable, which Jesus tells to answer the question: "'And who is my neighbor?'" [Luke 10:29]. Many of those who first heard this parable held Samaritans in great contempt, but Jesus makes a Samaritan the one who shows mercy. The person helped by the Samaritan is a man previously unknown to the Samaritan: a stranger who had been a victim of robbers and was left on the side of the road. Eighty-six percent of those completing the written survey agreed or strongly agreed that:

The parable of the Good Samaritan stands as a reminder that homosexual persons are our neighbors and should be treated with love and respect.

This parable has strong power to help people change their view of homosexual persons and of their responsibility toward homosexual persons. In our work with pilot congregations, we repeatedly found this parable to be an excellent way to help move undecided persons toward a warmer view of gay and lesbian people.

The written survey also asked clergy to indicate their level of agreement with this statement:

The creation passages in Genesis about the goodness of creation support a positive view of homosexuality as a part of creation.

Respondents were literally divided in their opinions about that item with exactly 50% indicating agreement or strong agreement and with 50% indicating disagreement or strong disagreement. The strength of opinion for those who agreed was stronger than for those who disagreed, with 37% saying they strongly agreed and only 12% saying they strongly disagreed.

In the telephone interviews, we found that most of those who had disagreed with that statement did so because they thought of the creation story telling of the formation of a man and of a woman and of the implication that the male-female relationship was the one which was more "natural" or "expected."

We also found in our work with pilot congregations that the biblical emphasis on hospitality has considerable power to motivate different attitudes and behaviors toward LGBT people. Passages like Genesis 18:1–15 and Hebrews 13:1–2 encourage showing hospitality to others, and those passages reflect the broad approach to hospitality that was taken in biblical times.

We also find that, for the most part, "relationships trump theology," which is to say that people can be won over emotionally through connecting with LGBT people and through hearing stories of their experiences that touch the heart. Fifty-seven percent of the clergy indicate that they have one or more close friends who are homosexual, and 29% have one or more members of the family who are homosexual. The clergy who have family members who are homosexual are much more likely to have progressive views on biblical interpretation! Close friends also had a significant influence.

Silent and Undecided Friends

We have had some helpful conversations with older clergy who draw comparisons between the current debates about homosexuality and debates decades ago about divorce. They point out to us that the minds of people on accepting divorced people into the congregation and as clergy changed when the tipping point was reached at which most people were connected personally to someone who had been divorced. *Then* they gave greater emphasis to biblical passages on grace and forgiveness and became able to accept those who had been divorced.

Here are some comments from clergy about the Scriptures and homosexuality:

Well, I'm not sure that you can go too far down the road of saying that the Scriptures support homosexuality as a variation in creation. But they sure don't support the attitude of hate and resentment toward gay people that so many seem to have. Even those of us who are opposed to homosexuality as a behavior should be preaching about the in of hatred. Missouri Synod Lutheran Minister

Completing that written survey actually had an influence on me. I know that wasn't your intention, but it did. I started thinking about the item about the goodness of creation, and for the first time it hit me that there have always been homosexual people, so that surely must be some part of God's overall plan. If that's the case, then why should we be so negative about it? Moravian Minister

I know this isn't original with me, but I think the Scriptures make a distinction between orientation and behavior. God did make us in such a way that some people are attracted to the same sex. But the Scriptures also tell us not to practice homosexual behavior. The orientation isn't a sin, but the behavior is. Brethren in Christ Minister

The parable of the Good Samaritan with the Samaritan representing the gay or lesbian person, that's a story with power. You can preach that. If Jesus were to tell that parable in our time, he probably would identify the hero as a gay man rather than as a Samaritan. Black Baptist Church Minister

We all look at the Bible through a certain set of lenses, and that affects what we see and what we conclude. Before my daughter told me that she was a lesbian, I had always taken the passages against homosexuality at face value. I didn't feel anger toward gay or lesbian people, but I thought they shouldn't engage in sexual activities. Then I learned that my daughter was a lesbian, and I started looking at the Bible in a new way. I gave more attention to the historical context of the clobber passages, and I put a whole lot more emphasis on all the passages about love and acceptance. And I realized that love and acceptance are always the final word in Scripture. We forget that sometimes. Nazarene Church Minister

Congregational Acceptance

We found considerable diversity in the perception of clergy on the welcome that homosexual persons can receive in the congregation and on whether or not that welcome is contingent on celibacy and on conversion to a heterosexual orientation. Those who responded to the written survey can be divided in this way:

- 41% Agreed or strongly agreed that homosexual persons can find welcome and acceptance in their congregation. *(No condition.)*

- 18% Agreed or strongly agreed that homosexual persons can find welcome and acceptance in their congregation *if* they are celibate.

- 12% Agreed or strongly agreed that homosexual persons can find welcome and acceptance in their congregation *if* they are celibate *and* are working to change to a heterosexual orientation.

- 21% Disagreed or strongly disagreed that homosexual persons can find welcome and acceptance in their congregation.

- 8% Expressed no opinion as to whether or not homosexual persons can find welcome and acceptance in their congregation.

Thus we find a total of 71% of the respondents feeling that homosexual persons can find welcome and acceptance in the congregation, but for some that welcome and acceptance are contingent on celibacy and in some instances even on working to change to a heterosexual orientation. **Thus only 41% of the respondents indicated an unqualified welcome.**

Fifty-seven percent of the surveyed clergy *personally* agree or strongly agree that homosexual persons should be fully welcomed and accepted as members and participants in the life of the church without qualification. The fact that 16% of the responding clergy personally support full acceptance without qualification but are in congregations that they do not perceive ready to grant that full acceptance suggests that there may be room for these clergy to have greater influence.

In addition to the 57% of clergy supporting welcome and acceptance without qualification, another 19% of the clergy support welcome and acceptance but qualify it with the desire for celibacy or for active work to change to a heterosexual orientation.

The above figures both for congregations and for clergy varied considerably depending on the denominational background of the person responding to the survey. Among United Methodist clergy, for example, 68% personally felt homosexual persons should be fully welcomed and accepted without qualification with another 23% qualifying that acceptance with the desire for celibacy or for active work to change to a heterosexual orientation. Among the African Methodist Episcopal Church clergy, only 21% personally supported welcome and acceptance without qualification; another 18% supported welcome and acceptance contingent on celibacy or active work to change orientation.

Both the written surveys and the phone interviews made it clear that many clergy really have no idea how many gay or lesbian members or constituents, if any, they have. Respondents to the written survey can be divided in this way:

- 32% Agreed or strongly agreed that there are homosexual persons who are currently participating in the life of the congregation.

- 24% Disagreed or strongly disagreed that there are homosexual persons who are currently participating in the life of the congregation.

- 44% Indicated that they do not know if there are homosexual persons who are currently participating in the life of the congregation.

Silent and Undecided Friends

Thirty-seven percent of the respondents to the written survey think there are persons in the congregation who are homosexual but that they are not open about it. As shared earlier, the written survey did not specifically ask about bisexual or transgender members or constituents. In the phone interviews, almost none felt that they had bisexual or transgender members; many of those clergy, however, readily acknowledged that they really didn't know.

Only 7% of the written respondents indicated that their congregation has gone on record as being open and affirming toward homosexual persons. With only a few exceptions, those congregations are in denominations that have active welcoming and accepting organizations working for change.

Here are some comments from clergy about the extent of the welcome in their congregations:

I'm afraid this congregation operates on the military "don't ask-don't tell" principle. We aren't negative about homosexuality, but we also aren't affirming. That makes people unwilling to divulge homosexual orientation or behavior. Yet we have three same-sex couples in this church that I and many others assume are homosexual. American Baptist Minister

I think the majority of the people in the congregation either feel positive toward gays or simply don't understand what it means to be homosexual. There are a few people who are negative but not many. United Methodist Minister

Our church has been very open and affirming of gay and lesbian people. And some of our growth in recent years has been through gay and lesbian people who've felt comfortable here. United Church of Christ Minister

Initially many people in our church were uncomfortable about the idea of having homosexual people involved. Then we had a young adult who had grown up in the church who came out as gay. That started changing things. So many people knew and loved this young man, and it just wasn't possible for them to be rude to him or to be rude to his parents. That created some openness to learning more about homosexuality and to taking another look at the biblical passages that condemn it. People started seeing the context of those passages, and they started paying more attention to all the biblical passages about love and acceptance. Now we have at least a dozen gay couples in the church, and it's really enriched us. We also have a number of heterosexual people who are strong gay rights advocates. Disciples of Christ Minister

Our congregation had many people who were initially uncomfortable when the denomination elected a gay bishop. But the younger people were more liberal about it, and the older people have been Episcopal so long that it's difficult for them to get too down on the denomination. The conversations proved very helpful, and I started to feel like I could preach more about sexuality in general and about homosexuality in particular. We're much more open now, and we've had some gay people join the church. We also had a couple who were lesbian who had been in the congregation for a decade who decided it was safe to be open about their orientation. Episcopal Priest

Things in our church really changed because of this wonderful woman in her sixties who started pushing her Sunday school class to talk more about sexuality. She got people in the class talking and thinking about LGBT rights and the Bible, and that class has some of the leaders of the church. Other classes decided to do the same study and asked her to teach it. It created openness, and now we reach out to gay and lesbian people just like we do to any other prospective members. We have several gay and lesbian people in the church. Evangelical Lutheran Minister

Two of our members have a son who came out as gay, and they got the church to offer an evening study on homosexuality. They encouraged people on the church board to take part in the study, and several of them did. By the end of the study, people in the class had decided that they wanted us as a church to become an open and safe place for homosexual people. But they weren't comfortable with a statement that singled out gays as a specific group who were welcome in our church. They felt that we needed a statement that showed a broad hospitality for

Silent and Undecided Friends

our congregation. We came up with this one: **First Baptist extends a warm welcome and the love of Christ to all people, regardless of gender, physical disability, ethnic background, economic level, or sexual orientation. Whatever your experiences in other churches, you will find warmth and acceptance in our congregation.** American Baptist Minister

Concern about Youth

Ministers who at first seem rather rigid in their disapproval of homosexual behavior begin to soften considerably when the subject of teens is raised with them. Christian Community has, from other re-search that we have done, significant data about what LGBT teens have experienced in congregational life, and we are finding that information very useful in talking with clergy.

The Christian Community book *Faith Matters: Teenagers, Sexuality, and Religion,* shares the results of a national study of 5,819 teens who are involved in their congregations. The study included Roman Catholic, mainline Protestant, evangelical Protestant, Anabaptist, Unitarian Universalist, Jewish, and Islamic teens. Because this information proved so valuable in the pilot work we have done with congregations on LGBT issues, we are sharing some of the data in this section of this report. For a fuller discussion, see the book *Faith Matters*.

If we had a preconceived idea of what we would find about the sexual orientation of teens who were involved in faith-based institutions, it was that we would likely discover a smaller percentage of teens self-identifying as homosexual or bisexual than has been found in secular studies. Our assumption was that teens of homosexual or bisexual orientation would be somewhat less likely to be involved in a faith-based institution, given the number of traditions with a negative view of homosexuality.

In looking at the results, it's important to be aware that forming a sexual identity is a developmental task of the adolescent years. Some sexuality education professionals report that as many as 25% of twelve-year-olds are unsure of their sexual orientation but that only 5% of eighteen-year-olds have that same uncertainty.

What we found, in fact, was that a surprisingly high number of teenagers who are involved in faith-based institutions self-identified as homosexual or bisexual. In fact most secular studies have reported lower percentages of teens who self-identify with homosexual or bisexual orientation than we found. As we have

Silent and Undecided Friends

shared the results with clergy and other congregational leaders, most have been surprised by the percentage of teens who didn't identify a heterosexual orientation. Remember that these figures reflect self-identification of orientation, not behavior:

	Males	Females
Heterosexual	86%	89%
Homosexual	7%	5%
Bisexual	5%	4%
Don't know	2%	2%

Those figures are among the highest percentages of gay, lesbian, and bisexual teens that have been identified in any study. We do not necessarily conclude from this that congregational teens are more likely than secular teens to be gay, lesbian, or bisexual. We do think that the way in which our study was conducted made it more likely for teens to feel safe in expressing their sexual orientation than has been the case in some other studies. Studies, for example, that rely on telephone interviews of teens are very likely to find gay, lesbian, and bisexual orientation and behavior under-reported. There has also been a recent trend toward teens not wanting to identify themselves by any particular orientation, though that is not reflected in our surveys or interviews from the 2000–2001 *Faith Matters* study.

What the *Faith Matters* study does clearly show is that most congregations have some teens who self-identify as gay, lesbian, or bisexual. There are also teens who are unsure about their orientation. Many of these teens have concerns both about how to relate their sexual orientation to their faith and about how accepted they would be if their sexual orientation were known by the congregation. For example:

> *I'm about as deep in the closet as a homosexual can be. My parents don't know. No one in my youth group knows. Almost no one at school knows. This other guy and I have been good friends since second grade. When we were in the fifth grade, we'd touch each other. Then we started to do other things and liked it. . . . Neither one of us is all that attracted to girls. We're careful not to hang out with each other too much at school. And fortunately our parents don't think anything about our*

spending time together in our rooms because we've always been friends. . . . Both of us are thinking we should ask girls to the prom. It isn't exactly fair to them in one way, but we'd probably be asking people who wouldn't get to go if not with us. . . . Kids at church and our youth advisor make these jokes about fags and queers. I'd never be accepted there if they knew I was gay. Junior—Southern Baptist Church

The only person in my synagogue who knows I'm bisexual is the girl that started doing things with me. . . . I think our rabbi believes that Jewish people are never homosexual—that it's like a condition that only Gentiles can get. . . . I just took for granted that I was a heterosexual when I was in middle school and a freshman. I dated and made out, and I loved doing that. . . . Then this friend and I were staying overnight, and we started talking about how the guys we dated didn't know how to touch you right. And we started doing things to each other, and it was great. I still like guys too, but it isn't possible for me to have as much pleasure with a guy as with her. . . . I think that many people have a homosexual side to them, but they bury it because society disapproves. . . . I can't decide whether God cares about my being bi. Senior—Synagogue

We found that almost all the congregations participating in the *Faith Matters* study had at least one teen who self-identified as gay, lesbian, bi-sexual, or questioning his or her orientation. **Eighty-six percent of those teens, however, said that their clergyperson was not aware of their orientation or their struggle; 46% of them indicated that their parents did not know about their orientation or their struggle.** When we surveyed the clergy in those congregations, only 18% thought that they had one or more LGBT teens in the congregation, and only 12% knew the name of a gay or lesbian teen.

Most of these teens do have at least one young person in the faith-based institution who knows about their orientation, so they are not completely isolated. Eighty-three percent indicated that there was at least one young person in the faith-based institution who was aware of their orientation, but only 16% said that the whole youth group or class knew about it. Very few of them have felt sufficiently comfortable to "come out" to their entire youth group or class.

Silent and Undecided Friends

Non-heterosexual teens in our study were almost twice as likely as heterosexual teens to have seriously considered suicide. This should be a matter of significant concern for those of us in faith-based institutions. And almost all the clergy with whom we visited in the interviews as part of the process leading to the report you are reading right now indicated that they are very concerned about this fact.

There have been some recent secular studies indicating that non-heterosexual teens may not be as much at risk for suicide and depression as previously thought. We wonder if it is possible that the risk for religious teens is slightly higher because of the frequent conflict between their perceived orientation and the teachings of their congregation.

If the teens perceived that their pastor or another adult in the church felt "open, accepting, or nonjudgmental" about matters of sexual orientation, they were much more likely to have talked with someone in the congregation about the topic. Those who were able to be open in their faith-based communities were also less likely to have considered suicide than other non-heterosexual teens in this study. Those who are in faith-based institutions where there are negative views toward homosexuality and bisexuality rarely are open about their orientation. Those teens live with a very painful silence.

In our focus groups, clergy and adult leaders from traditions which disapprove of homosexuality were struck by the high percentage of teens in this study who have non-heterosexual orientation. Almost all of them acknowledged the importance of being more open so that these teens can talk about issues of orientation in religious settings. Having that kind of openness, however, is very difficult when people are in a faith tradition that teaches that homosexuality is a sin. One African Methodist Episcopal pastor shared the dilemma in this way:

I am very sorry that I came here tonight, and I am very glad that I came here tonight. I am sorry because my life would have been a lot simpler without learning these things. We have a big youth group. And what I hear you saying is that we've got to have some gay and lesbian kids in that group. I'm glad I came because I can see that we need to do something about this. I think homosexual behavior is a sin, but it's clear that these kids aren't choosing their homosexual orientation. So what do we want them to do? Be celibate forever? Become heterosexual? I mean, their becoming heterosexual would be the solution for the church, but is that possible? . . . We simply have to find ways to talk with these kids. We've got to let them know that we don't blame them for an orientation and that God loves them and wants to help them. But how do we convey that when we see the behavior as a sin?

Pastors of predominantly black congregations were more likely to disapprove of homosexual behavior than pastors in congregations with other ethnic compositions. The youth in those congregations were also more likely to indicate that their congregation disapproved of homosexual behavior. Black clergy in our focus groups in the *Faith Matters* study said that they felt it was even more difficult to talk about homosexuality in a black congregation than in a white congregation and that it was difficult to talk about any sexually related topic in their churches.

A pastor in the United Methodist Church shared a very interesting perspective:

Think about what it says that there are so many kids in our churches who are gay and who aren't open about it. If I were gay and felt disapproval from the church, I'd stop coming. But most of these young people are continuing to be active. That says to me that God and the church are very important to them.

The United Methodist pastor was absolutely right. Religious faith and involvement in faith-based institutions are very important for the young people in the *Faith Matters* study who have a non-heterosexual orientation. We found no differences between heterosexual and non-heterosexual teens in the importance they placed on religion in their lives, on their commitment to God, on their frequency of prayer, or on their commitment to the congregation.

Ninety-six percent of the teens who completed surveys for this study indicate that they know at least one person their age (or within two years of their age) who has a gay, lesbian, or bisexual orientation. Most know several such persons. The 4% who indicated that they do not tended to be in more rural areas. While many teens who have such an orientation are reluctant to share that in their congregation much further than with one or two especially close friends, almost all teens know someone their age who is gay, lesbian, or bisexual. This is a part of life for teenagers today, and it is a part of life which congregations need to recognize.

Some of the teens who participated in the *Faith Matters* study have a parent who is involved in a homosexual relationship. We did not include a direct item about the sexual orientation of parents in the survey, but the written comments and interview comments of teens make it clear that such situations are not rare. Some of the teens with a parent who is openly gay feel awkwardness and a little embarrassment about it, but most indicated that they have come to accept the orientation.

Focusing on youth concerns is a strong starting point for further work in this area, and this is the starting point most frequently chosen by the pilot congregations. Consider the percentage of clergy in our current study who agreed or strongly agreed with these statements (these figures are from the current study on which this report is based rather than from the earlier *Faith Matters* study):

91% People in the congregation would be concerned to know that the suicide rate for homosexual teens is twice the rate for heterosexual teens.

81% The church is capable of becoming more understanding and helpful toward teens who are homosexual or struggling with identifying a sexual orientation.

Obviously in a conservative or fundamentalist congregation, one could be concerned that a greater awareness of the potential presence of gay and lesbian teens would result in efforts to identify them and to try to change their orientation. The clergy in our study, however, were primarily moderate and progressive. When they became aware in phone interviews of the percentage of teens in congregations who have self-identified as gay, lesbian, or bisexual, many saw this as further evidence that people do not so much "choose" an orientation as simply "have" an orientation.

Motivating Greater LGBT Rights Advocacy

The pilot congregations with which we worked on creating greater LGBT acceptance were more likely to start work with teens, youth workers, and parents than with any other single category or strategy. The full manual being developed out of this study gives considerable detail on the strategies used. Here's a brief overview of some of the things congregations did:

- Studies of the book *Faith Matters* by parents, youth teachers, and youth group advisors. The book helps them better understand how teens relate their sexuality to their faith and provides considerable information about non-heterosexual teens.

- Studies of *The Gift of Sexuality* in youth classes and groups. That book is a very progressive look at sexuality and faith for teens and includes a very positive view of gay and lesbian teens.

- Adopting a statement about the youth program in the church being open to all young people including those of LGBT orientation. These churches sought to become safe places for LGBT youth, and their teens actively encouraged LGBT youth they knew to participate in church activities.

- Having a study of *Faith Matters* open to the congregation as a whole to help them better understand issues of youth and sexuality, including those of LGBT youth.

- Incorporating information about LGBT teens, including suicide rates, into sermons and newsletter articles as a means of raising awareness.

All of these are strategies which have the impact of increasing the number of people in the church with a better understanding of LGBT concerns and with greater openness to LGBT people.

Our pilot work was entirely with congregations in the moderate category. When our telephone interviews were with clergy who turned out to be more conservative than we had anticipated, we nevertheless found them to be considerably softer in their views of LGBT youth than in their other positions on LGBT concerns.

Silent and Undecided Friends

Having conservative clergy more fully informed on LGBT teens would appear to be a useful strategy, but we have not pursued that further at the present time. We do have the concern that making them more aware of those teens might result in efforts to identify and "change" those teens, which is not something we want to encourage.

Welcoming and Affirming Organizations

Many denominations have what are often called Welcoming and Affirming organizations that are working both for greater acceptance of LGBT persons in congregations and for denominational policies that support the rights of LGBT persons, including the right to licensing and ordination for ministry.

Some of these groups have been in existence for many years, and the emphasis of some groups has changed over time. Initially some of them primarily provided programs, opportunities, and settings that gave safe places or sanctuary to LGBT persons. While that function still continues for some of these groups, work on congregational acceptance and on denominational justice issues have become of increasing importance.

It seems to us significant that virtually all the clergy we surveyed in denominations that have such groups were aware of the existence of the group and of their mission. Because these groups are working for justice in their denominations and are in some instances pushing clergy and congregations to deal with LGBT concerns, it's not surprising that some clergy have strong feelings about the groups. There are clergy who are deeply supportive of their work, there are clergy who are opposed to their work, and there are also clergy who are made uncomfortable by their work.

Many clergy who are personally supportive of the work of these groups are not willing to align with them in a public way. That was clearly shown in the responses to the written survey (which follow) and in the telephone interviews.

For the purpose of these percentages, we have taken out the responses of United Church of Christ and Unitarian Universalist clergy since those denominations are on record as fully accepting of LGBT persons and the groups in those denominations working on LGBT issues are connected in a different way to the official structure. As would be expected, feelings about the denominational groups were more positive in those denominations.

Silent and Undecided Friends

We have also excluded from these percentages the small number of responses from respondents in denominations that had no clearly identifiable welcoming and affirming organization and also no clear connection with a multi-denominational group. Most of those respondents checked "no opinion" or left the item blank.

Here are the percentages of respondents to the written survey who agreed or strongly agreed with each statement. Each of these statements appeared separately on the written survey, so the responses total more than 100%.

39% I am personally supportive of the organization (or organizations) in the denomination that are working to create greater acceptance of homosexual persons.

36% I think the organization (or organizations) in the denomination that are working to create greater acceptance of homosexual persons are serving a needed function, but I do not feel I can lend support to them at the present time.

48% I think the organization (or organizations) in the denomination that are working to create greater acceptance of homosexual persons are currently doing more harm than good.

14% I have shown or am willing to show public support for the organization (or organizations) in the denomination that are working to create greater acceptance of homosexual persons.

The 48% who feel the organizations are currently doing more harm than good were not necessarily opposed to greater LGBT welcome and acceptance in congregations. The phone interviews suggest to us that some clergy were simply reflecting their own lack of comfort dealing with LGBT concerns, and some were reflecting honest misgivings about the role of the group in their denomination. It's also important to note that 52% of the respondents did not agree with that statement.

Motivating Greater LGBT Rights Advocacy

The LGBT rights groups within denominations are perceived by some clergy as being managed and influenced primarily by gay and lesbian persons, who are perceived as having a personal "agenda." Several clergy indicated in phone interviews that these groups need more visible heterosexual allies, though not all who said that were willing to be those allies!

The negative responses to those groups from some clergy bring to mind Matthew 5:11-12 in *The Message* version:

> Not only that—count yourselves blessed every time people put you down or throw you out or speak lies about you to discredit me. What it means is that the truth is too close for comfort and they are uncomfortable. You can be glad when that happens—give a cheer, even!—for though they don't like it, I do! And all heaven applauds. And know that you are in good company. My prophets and Witnesses have always gotten into this kind of trouble.

"The truth is too close for comfort and they are uncomfortable" says it well. Were the welcoming and advocacy groups not having impact, there would not be such strong feelings about them. And in many instances they are indeed making silent progressives and moderates uncomfortable because they are bringing the truth about LGBT acceptance and justice too close for comfort!

Our phone interviews made us more deeply aware of the distinction between the strategies and skills needed to work for greater acceptance of LGBT people at the congregational level and the strategies and skills needed for advocacy work at the denominational level. Though some measure of confrontation may be involved in working for a warmer welcome and greater acceptance of LGBT people within congregations, it must be a very gentle confrontation if it is to be effective rather than simply turning people off. Force and pressure do not do much to warm the hearts of people!

At the denominational level, however, there are times when assertive confrontation is necessary in the process of working for justice on matters such as licensing and ordination. In one denomination, for example, the Program and Arrangements

Silent and Undecided Friends

Committee has for decades refused exhibit space at annual meetings to the Council for LGBT Interests. That refusal has continued even though a very conservative group with the same kind of unofficial connection to the denomination has been granted exhibit space every year. There are past and present members of that Committee that acknowledge the injustice in this but who still continue to vote against granting exhibit space to the Council. In the face of this, there is no good alternative to working the church political system and confronting the injustice of the continued exclusion.

When advocacy groups become identified at the denominational level as pushing hard for those kinds of reform, they can be perceived as being polarizing and as having an "agenda." Justice certainly does constitute an agenda. The perceptions related to this denominational advocacy carry over into the feelings of clergy when approached by these groups for more work on welcome and acceptance at the congregational level. Some clergy shared in interviews that they understood themselves the distinction between the approaches and skills needed in work at the denominational level and at the congregational level but that the denominational advocacy had turned off many of the lay persons in their congregations.

The distinction between the approaches needed for congregational work and for denominational work create a bind for the people in the welcoming and affirming groups. Both kinds of work are very important, and it is unfortunate that the push for justice at the denominational level causes difficulty gaining entrance to congregations for welcoming and affirming work.

Obviously success in securing licensing and ordination rights for LGBT persons at the denominational level will in time open more doors in congregations for work on welcoming and acceptance. There is significant anecdotal evidence that this has happened in many instances in the United Church of Christ. And United Church of Christ clergy responding to our written survey reflected a more positive view of those working for LGBT rights than was present in other Protestant denominations. Certainly an increase in the number of congregations who are welcoming and affirming of LGBT persons helps create a broader base of people willing to work for justice at the denominational level. Thus the two areas of work unquestionably, in the long run, reinforce each other. The distinction while this work is in process, however, is part of the reason that some clergy are uncomfortable with the welcoming and affirming groups.

Though there are some unhealthy congregations that seem to thrive on internal discord and conflict, a tremendous number of congregations and their ministers want to avoid discord and conflict if at all possible. Christian Community has extensive experience working with clergy at the congregational level, and we find very few clergy who are comfortable living with differences of opinion or conflict. Most also do not feel that they have the necessary skills to deal with conflict.

Conflict is a part of community life, and our congregations are people living in community. Complete avoidance of discord and conflict is not realistic unless some people simply choose to repress their true beliefs and opinions. The topic of homosexuality is one on which people of good faith do not always agree. It is almost impossible for a congregation to work at becoming more welcoming and affirming of LGBT people without there being at least some dissent in the congregation. Clergy fear that dissent and want to avoid the conflict that they fear may result from it. Yet healthy congregations are able to deal with some differences of opinion.

Many of the clergy with whom we visited fear that the involvement of a denominational welcoming and affirming group or the use of their resources will raise an uncomfortable level of conflict in the congregation. Many of them also fear that representatives of the welcoming and affirming group will be abrasive and confrontational in their work with the congregation because they have observed them being, in their opinion, abrasive and confrontational at the denominational level. This fear, while based largely on misperceptions of how the welcoming and affirming group would function in work at the congregational level, is very real. In fact it is so real that when doing the telephone interviews, we sometimes had to reassure the minister we were calling that we did not have any connection with the welcoming and affirming group in the denomination before he or she would be willing to talk with us.

Silent and Undecided Friends

It's also important to keep perspective here. Remember that while 48% of those who completed our written survey indicated a feeling that the welcoming and affirming groups are doing more harm than good, 52% did not feel that way. Many of the clergy with whom we visited who were not yet willing to be public in their support, nevertheless indicated great appreciation for the courage of the leaders of these groups and for the importance of what they are doing. They are indeed silent friends, and we need to motivate them to become more public in their support.

A few of the statements from clergy about the welcoming and affirming groups follow. For the most part here, as in the rest of this report, I've not used the actual names of people, but in a couple of instances I couldn't resist doing so. With a few of the statements that are especially critical of welcoming and affirming groups, I've chosen not to reveal the denomination involved.

People like Ruth Garwood and Mike Schuenemeyer in my denomination are my heroes. They've been a major part of making it happen in the United Church of Christ. We still have a long way to go before we have full acceptance at the congregational level, but people like them have blazed the trail and had the courage to speak out. United Church of Christ Minister

Here in the middle of Wisconsin, we don't much care what the people in Cleveland decide to do or to recommend or what action gets taken at the national level. People in my church are not even close to being ready to be accepting of homosexual people. I wish it weren't that way, but I'd lose my job and the church would lose a lot of money if I started pushing the issue. United Church of Christ Minister [The Cleveland" reference is to the national offices of the denomination which are in Cleveland.]

We've taken some good steps as a denomination. The willingness to have a gay bishop wouldn't have happened if people hadn't been building the base of welcoming and affirming people. I think Integrity has had considerably greater impact that people realize. The number of formal members and

supporters of the organization isn't an accurate measure of its influence. Episcopal Priest

There's a battle going on in the United Methodist Church. There are the Reconciling people who are pushing as hard as they can for full acceptance including ordination, and there are the conservatives working hard to prevent it. I feel like these people are shooting at each other, and I have no desire to get caught in the crossfire. And the differences on this issue aren't like there are ten thousand churches that are gay friendly and another ten thousand that aren't. For the most part, the differences in opinion go right down the middle of almost every congregation. There's no way I want a battle in the church I pastor like the battle in the denomination. United Methodist Minister

To tell you the truth, I feel ashamed. When I was a seminary student, I worked for racial justice and for peace. I don't pretend to know everything I should about why some people are homosexual or bisexual, but I'm real clear on how God wants us to treat everyone. And some of the gay people in the denomination are among the finest people I know. I'm also sure there are at least half-a-dozen gay people in my congregation, though they aren't open about it. But I've pretty much kept my mouth shut. My local church has been losing members for twenty years, and I haven't been able to reverse the trend. I know I should be more open in support, but frankly I'm afraid to do it. I admire the people who are more open in their support, and I know I should do more. United Methodist Minister

Our coming out in full support of gay and lesbian people was one of the best things we've done in our [local] *church. I was afraid we might lose a few member over it, but the reverse is what's happened. We've gained members who are gay and lesbian, and we've also gained heterosexual people who are concerned about justice. The Reconciling Ministries Network is the most undervalued organization in the denomination.* United Methodist Minister

Silent and Undecided Friends

More Light has done a lot of good, but there are people in my congregation who are afraid of them. They see the conflict at the national level, and they don't want it happening in our church. I think we can make some progress on gay and lesbian acceptance, but we'll have to do it on our own. Presbyterian Minister

Emily Eastwood is one of the smartest people I know. Our denomination wouldn't have made most of the progress we have on gay and lesbian issues without the really strategic way she works. She has great influence at the denominational level and at the local church level. Evangelical Lutheran Minister

I'm sorry I seemed evasive at the start of the call. I was afraid you were with [name of the denominational advocacy group], and I was frankly nervous about what you'd do with any information that I gave you. We are at the point in our denomination where the group is doing more harm than good. I agree that we need to be doing more for acceptance of homosexual people. I also agree that a gay man or woman should be able to be ordained the same as anyone else. But I think the work at the congregational level has to be done by the people in the church, maybe with the help of some group that isn't perceived as being so polarizing. Minister

The group in my denomination has no standing at all. In general, I think that black churches are slower than white churches to accept homosexual people. At least my denomination has been slow. I would say we have maybe 10% of our pastors who accept homosexuals and don't think it's a sin. We have maybe 40 or 50% who are sure it's a sin and that homosexuals are going to hell. The others are undecided. They feel warm toward the gay people they know, but they don't know what to do with the Scriptures. Minister

Ministers in my denomination are starting to get past identifying AIDS just with people who are gay. For a long time, people thought it was just a gay problem and maybe brought on as a punishment. Now that so many young people of both sexes in our churches are getting it, it isn't possible to keep saying it's just a gay issue. I think that shift has helped people feel more

Motivating Greater LGBT Rights Advocacy

positive toward gay people and less afraid of them. There are a couple of groups working for acceptance of gays in black churches, and I think they're having an impact. Some of us resent being pushed by them, but I appreciate what they're doing. Minister

People look at [name of the denominational advocacy group] *and think it's just a group of gay people with an agenda. People in those groups want to be accepted and ordained and able to be married, but they aren't concerned about the greater good of the church. It's going to take another twenty years for gays to be fully accepted in our society. There's no way to hurry that process. And when you push the church too hard, it backfires. I'm for full equality for gay people but with the war in Iraq and all the people who are hungry, I just don't think it's the most important issue on the table.* Minister

I think [name of the denominational advocacy group] *has done some good nationally. They've made us look at homosexuality as a justice issue. But I think they make a mistake in working with clergy and churches at the local level when they make the "acid test" of commitment to gay and lesbian rights and acceptance be whether or not a church is willing to adopt their statement and be listed on their website. I understand all the reasons why they say that gay and lesbian people need the reassurance of a public statement just for them rather than a broad statement of acceptance of all people. But my church would be far more likely to adopt a broad statement that included gay and lesbian people. And a study on broad-based hospitality would be easier to implement and would have better attendance, ultimately helping gay and lesbian concerns.* Minister

[Name of the denominational advocacy group] *would be more effective if the group didn't seem to be made up almost entirely of gay people, certainly that's the way its leadership is. They need more heterosexual people working to help them. I think they would get into a lot more churches if their staff person was heterosexual instead of gay. People expect that gay people are going to be for gay rights. They listen more when a heterosexual person talks about gay rights.* Minister

Silent and Undecided Friends

> *I respect the director of* [name of denominational advocacy group], *and I sometimes feel guilty for not being more supportive. At the same time, I think she has no idea how she comes across when she talks to people at our national meetings or in the congregations. She comes across as so angry. I understand the anger. If I were gay and still waiting for full equality, I'd be angry too. But people are driven away by the anger. We aren't going to change the typical person in the local church until we learn how to make the approach out of love.* Minister

> *People in* [name of the denominational advocacy group] *don't understand that the people who are opposed to gay rights aren't evil people. They're just acting consistently with how they understand the Bible and the faith. What happens is that both sides of this debate try to portray the other side as unchristian. I don't think that's true. I don't think there are any bad people or unfaithful people here. There are just people on both sides who have a different view of the issue. But I'm telling you that the anger that comes across from* [name of the denominational advocacy group] *sounds just like that from the people opposed to gay rights. If the people in that* [advocacy] *group could learn how to approach people with greater respect and greater love, they'd be surprised how much better a hearing they'd get.* Minister

> *I know the director of* [name of the denominational advocacy group] *thinks that people like me just don't care. But what a lot of people don't realize is how great a load the typical minister carries and how many causes and organizations are wanting the minister to help them out. Are equal rights for homosexual people more important than feeding the poor? Are those rights more important than protecting the environment? There's so much need in the church and outside the church with people killed in Iraq, people starving even in this country, and the environment being destroyed. Some of us simply find it hard to take on homosexual issues when there are so many things that need to be done. I'm not saying it isn't important. It is. And it's vitally important to those who are gay and lesbian. But making it a priority isn't easy.* Minister

Evangelicals like me are pretty much associated with opposition to gay rights. That's going to change, and I'll tell you why. Being against gay rights is being on the wrong side of the issue, and it's going to keep separating us from young adults who are much more progressive on this issue. There really is self-gain involved here in taking a more accepting attitude toward gay and lesbian people. Congregations that do this are going to be the ones that grow over the next twenty years. They'll reach gay and lesbian people and their families, and they'll also reach more young adults. The evangelical groups working for greater LGBT acceptance should be helping people see the self-gain in more open and affirming policies. They keep approaching it as an issue of justice when they should approach it as an issue of self-gain. Minister

Christian Community has great respect for all of the welcoming and affirming groups including those within specific denominations and those working across denominations. We are convinced that the work of these groups is very important and that the groups need more allies both through individuals and organizations. The Institute for Welcoming Resources brings together the groups from several major Protestant denominations, sharing resources and strategies. Each group working within a specific denomination knows their own congregations and the hierarchy in a deeper way than Christian Community can as an outside organization that works with a large number of different congregations and denominations. On the basis of our survey work and our interviews with clergy, we offer the following suggestions, knowing that they will not apply in every situation.

1. Our interviews show that more visible heterosexual allies would be an asset to the image of these groups with many moderate clergy. We recognize that many LGBT people have been disappointed by heterosexuals who claim to be allies but don't always remain firm in their advocacy in the face of conflict. More heterosexual allies with a true commitment to justice for LGBT people would help the cause, and those allies do need to be visible.

If you are reading this report and can self-identify as a silent friend of LGBT people, we want to encourage you to consider the possibility that you should become more public

Silent and Undecided Friends

in your support. The influence of the welcoming and affirming organizations will greatly increase with the addition of more heterosexual allies.

2. There are some movable clergy and congregations who, for a variety of reasons (many of which are unfair), are not going to be reached or influenced primarily by the welcoming and affirming organizations in the denominations. There is a need for parachurch organizations like Christian Community; the Religious Institute on Sexual Morality, Justice, and Healing; the Human Rights Campaign; the National Gay and Lesbian Task Force; and Progressive Christians Uniting to seek more opportunities to influence congregations. Groups doing this work need to be in as close partnership as possible with the welcoming and affirming organizations in the denominations.

Other organizations within denominations that are concerned about justice issues also need to be enlisted in more visible efforts on behalf of LGBT acceptance and rights. This includes groups that are concerned about social justice, peace issues, and even church growth. We'll have more to say later in this report about the reasons why a positive view of LGBT people can actually contribute to the efforts of congregations to grow.

If greater LGBT acceptance can be encouraged in congregations by the efforts of parachurch organizations and by other denominational organizations, that will end up creating broader support for welcoming and accepting organizations within denominations. It's important that there be sufficient communication that these efforts by a variety of groups are not seen as competitive but rather as mutually reinforcing.

3. Leaders in the welcoming and affirming organizations do need to be aware that they and their groups are perceived as being angry and polarizing by some clergy. As shared earlier, this perception heavily grows out of the advocacy and justice work being done at the denominational level. That work needs to continue, and people who have been denied justice have a right to be angry about it. Where it is possible to show greater warmth in contacts with local clergy and congregations, doing so will help change the image of these groups in positive ways.

4. The welcoming and affirming groups and all others working for LGBT acceptance and justice need to do all that they can to help clergy and congregations begin to focus on what they are missing by not being more accepting of LGBT people. *Clergy are so focused on what they risk by being more proactive on behalf of LGBT people that they are generally oblivious to what they are losing by not being openly welcoming and affirming.*

Christian Community will be implementing a strategy beginning in 2008 which includes mailing clergy a booklet about the reasons why congregations need LGBT people involved, offering them a strategy manual, and following up with phone calls. We've based this model in large part on the strategies being used by some of the parachurch groups that are working against LGBT acceptance. We are interested in doing much of that mailing work in cooperation with denominational welcoming and affirming groups. Thus our organization can make the initial contacts, coach selected clergy, and then refer the clergy and congregations to the appropriate welcoming and affirming organization if appropriate.

5. As the welcoming and affirming groups are already aware, it's very important to tailor the approach with a particular congregation to the strategies most likely to be successful in that setting. Justice approaches, civil rights emphases, hospitality approaches, sexuality study approaches, and evangelism emphases can all be effective in some churches. While there certainly is benefit to organizing around core strategies and social marketing themes, no single approach is the one that will bring change in all congregations. We need tool kits with a variety of strategies.

6. While this is stating the obvious, it's important to remain aware that there is broader clergy and congregational support for LGBT acceptance and rights than is reflected in the actual number of congregations that sign on as open and affirming.

The welcoming and affirming organizations have done a good job articulating the reasons why LGBT people need the support of specific statements that clearly say they are welcome and included rather than of general statements about hospitality to all people. Many of the clergy whom we interviewed, however, were uncomfortable with the concept of statements and affiliations that

Silent and Undecided Friends

lifted up inclusion of LGBT persons without a comparable emphasis on persons of different economic levels, physical abilities, ethnic backgrounds, and so forth. In some instances, that lack of comfort no doubt reflects a waffling of commitment on LGBT issues and a fear of conflict; but there were many instances in which clergy were sharing a genuine philosophical concern. Both kinds of statements are valuable.

Integration into Broader Studies

Both the written survey and the interviews reinforced the reality that clergy and lay people need better factual information about a wide range of topics related to LGBT acceptance and to LGBT rights both within the church and within the larger society. We repeatedly encountered inadequate or erroneous information about sexual orientation, the Bible, transgender, laws concerning homosexuality, and other concerns.

Some congregations have done studies specifically on the topic of homosexuality, and those studies sometimes result in the decision of a congregation to become open and affirming. We did find that clergy were most open to approaches to education and change on these issues that integrated issues of sexual orientation into broader studies of human rights or of religion and sexuality. Consider the percentage of clergy who agreed or strongly agreed with the following statements:

- 23% Our church has had study groups which worked to better understand homosexuality.

- 34% Our church would not respond well to a study group on homosexuality.

- 74% I think our church would respond better to a study on human rights, including the rights of homosexuals, than to a study focused just on homosexuality.

- 82% I think our church would respond better to a study on religion and sexuality, including the topic of homosexuality, than to a study focused just on homosexuality.

There are many excellent studies on homosexuality that have been developed for use in congregations. There are also many excellent books that have been written on topics like homosexuality and the Bible. We need to be aware, however, that some clergy who are not yet ready to push a study focused primarily on

Silent and Undecided Friends

homosexuality are open to the topic being covered in a broader study. Several of the pilot congregations with which we worked chose to integrate a study of homosexuality into a broader study of human rights, of religion and sexuality, or of hospitality. The quality of the discussions on homosexuality generated by those approaches was very high.

The sixteen congregations that used the hospitality framework for their study all generated statements out of the study process that supported a broad hospitality that included people of all sexual orientations. The biblical passages on hospitality offer little "wiggle room" for excluding certain categories of people, and church members identify positively with the images of themselves as hospitable people.

A full discussion of the potential and the limitations of such integrated approaches goes beyond the scope of this report but is covered in the larger strategy manual that we have developed.

Some clergy feel as though the only way to talk about LGBT concerns in a sermon or in the worship service is by making that the focus of a sermon. Certainly there have been many sermons preached in North America that condemned homosexuality. Clergy who are supportive of a welcoming and affirming approach to LGBT people are not always confident about devoting a sermon to the defense of that position.

In our work with pilot congregations, we cooperated with several clergy on efforts to integrate LGBT concerns into sermons and worship in substantive ways that were comfortable for the minister and the congregation. We found that good starting points included:

- Using LGBT people as positive examples in sermons. By doing this, clergy help humanize LGBT people and also convey their own acceptance of LGBT people.

- Sharing with the congregation some of the discrimination that LGBT people face as examples of injustice.

- Including LGBT people and concerns in prayers and litanies.

- Using experiences of LGBT people when talking about the place of hospitality in the life of the church.

- Working to make the announcements and other worship language less heterosexist. Many statements get made in church that assume everyone present is in a heterosexual marriage with children. This not only makes LGBT people uncomfortable but also has that impact on any single people and on couples without children.

- Sharing information about LGBT youth as part of a sermon.

- Having bulletin inserts that talk about sexual orientation and related topics.

Starting with some of those strategies lays a foundation that makes it easier for the minister to talk in increasingly direct ways about the importance of true hospitality to LGBT people and about the importance of LGBT rights in both congregations and in the larger society.

We found the materials provided by the Out in Scripture emphasis of the Human Rights Campaign especially helpful to clergy in efforts to integrate these concerns into preaching and worship. Our strategy manual shares many specific examples of effective ways to deal with LGBT concerns in worship.

Affirmation of Civil Rights

Even clergy who are ambivalent about the involvement of homosexual persons within the life of the congregation reflect a commitment to the protection of the civil rights of homosexual persons. In fact the level of that commitment was much higher than we had anticipated prior to conducting the survey. Consider the percentages who agreed or strongly agreed with the following statements:

- 93% I support laws which protect the civil rights of homosexual persons.

- 62% I support civil unions for homosexual persons.

- 37% I support the right to marry for homosexual persons.

- 34% I think that giving the right to marry to homosexual persons would threaten the sanctity of marriage.

- 18% Depending on the couple (as with heterosexual couples), I would perform a civil union/marriage service for homosexual persons if such a service was legal where I was located.

- < 1% I have performed a civil union/marriage service for homosexual persons.

The broad agreement on the importance of support for laws protecting the civil rights of homosexual persons raises interesting possibilities for work with clergy and with congregations. In the telephone interviews, we discovered that most clergy were not aware of or had not thought about the number of inequities that exist in terms of protection under the laws of city, county, state, and federal governments. Here are some statements made about the civil rights of LGBT people:

Homosexuality isn't the unforgivable sin, and homosexual people are just as much children of God as anyone else. I believe that a Christian has a moral obligation to support the rights of all people. Missouri Synod Lutheran Minister

A couple in our church has a son who's gay and who has been with the same partner for almost twenty years. When his partner got hospitalized with cancer, their son found out that he had no legal rights at all concerning visiting or decision-making about his partner's care. That privilege went to his partner's parents who hadn't spoken to him for five years. There's something very wrong with this kind of system. American Baptist Minister

We have a wonderful lesbian couple in our congregation who were named the guardians of the niece and the nephew of one of them when a car accident killed the parents of the children. I've seen first-hand how loving and caring these people have been. They are better parents than most of the people in my congregation. But in my state, I don't think they could have gotten custody of children in any other circumstances than the family tie and the clear intent of the will of the parents. With so many children needing good homes, we should be encouraging homo-sexual couples to adopt. United Methodist Minister

We have a wonderful, deeply spiritual young man in our church who has told me he is gay. He keeps quiet about it because most of our people would disapprove, but I think a lot of folks know. He's been a very dedicated public school teacher. Last month he lost his job because it came out at the school that he was gay. There was no hearing. There was no due process. He was immediately fired. There wasn't even any real proof that he was gay; just the rumor was enough to do it. This is horribly wrong. Progressive Baptist Minister

She isn't a member of my church and almost never comes, but I have a friend who is a male-to-female trans. I admire the courage that she's shown, and I'm ashamed that I don't think she would be welcome in my church. . . . When she changed her name and her appearance, people where she worked were uncomfortable but tried to go along with it. Where she could go to the bathroom, however, became a big deal. The men didn't want a woman in a dress coming into their restroom, and the women didn't want her in theirs. There's no separate

> handicapped bathroom or male/female bathroom there. She kept insisting that she was a woman and should use the woman's restroom. It finally got her fired. By that time, she'd endured so many dirty looks and snide comments that it was almost a relief. But it was very wrong and cruel. Missionary Church Minister

Of course not every comment was positive, and the responses would no doubt have been different if our study had included more conservative clergy. There were also some clergy who were in a broad way supportive of civil rights but were less enthusiastic in interviews when topics as specific as adoption were raised. Nevertheless, this sample of progressive and moderate clergy was on the whole broadly supportive of the civil rights of LGBT people; and that fact should be considered in advocacy work.

Support for civil unions and for marriage equality was greater than we expected to find. Almost one out of five clergy said that they would perform a civil union/marriage service for homosexual persons if such a service was legal where they are located. Responding to an item on a survey is of course far less risky than actually doing a service, but we are encouraged that this many clergy would consider doing a civil union or marriage service for homosexual persons. Here are some of the comments that were made:

> I know that many ministers in my denomination would disagree, but I think civil unions ought to be legal for gay people. We talk about wanting them to have commitment, so why do we deny them the opportunity to express that? I would get a shit-load of criticism; but if it were legal and I felt good about the couple, I would do the service. Nazarene Minister

> It's cheap for me to say this because civil unions and gay marriage are both illegal in my state, but I absolutely would do the service if it was for people I respected. By that I don't mean any different criteria than for heterosexual people. If it was clear to me that they were committed and that their faith was important to them, I'd be honored to do the service.
> Presbyterian Minister

Although the ceremony doesn't have any legal standing in our state, I've performed commitment services for four gay couples. These have been among the most meaningful services I've ever performed. These are people with deep faith. People in my church haven't all been enthused about this, but they respect my right to do it. My bishop is supportive of it too when he talks to me privately. He won't make a public statement because he's afraid of losing financial support. Episcopal Priest

The distinction between a civil union and a marriage is important to me. Biblically, I just don't see how you can do a marriage for anything other than a man and a woman. But a civil union seems to me something different that still respects the rights and honors the love of people. I might get in a lot of trouble, but I think I would do the service if it became legal here. African Methodist Episcopal Minister

The right wing has done us a big disservice by convincing people that civil unions or gay marriage would somehow undermine the meaning of heterosexual marriage. I don't see how what two other people call their relationship has any impact on my marriage at all. If my marriage isn't good, it's not because gay people are able to get married. It's because my wife and I have a problem. Church of the Brethren Minister

Licensing and Ordination

The percentages of clergy supporting the licensing and ordination of homosexual persons as clergy varied considerably from denomination to denomination, ranging from 87% among United Church of Christ respondents, to 68% among United Methodists, to 48% among American Baptists, to 6% among Progressive Baptists. Here are some of the comments made about this:

> We've lost some very talented people out of our denomination because they couldn't be ordained. Some of these people had rich gifts for ministry that are completely lost. And this is in a time when we almost desperately need more clergy, at least in my part of the country. United Methodist Minister

> The licensing and ordination question is irrelevant right now. Until we have a greater acceptance of homosexual people in the pew, it doesn't matter. Right now there aren't enough churches that would even remotely consider a gay pastor. African Methodist Episcopal Zion Minister

> My denomination, with the acceptance of LGBT clergy, has gained a lot from the denominations that are more closed. We get gay clergy coming to us, and we also get heterosexual clergy that are tired of being in a denomination that discriminates. Many of these are outstanding clergy, and they are strengthening our denomination. United Church of Christ Minister

> I think our denomination is about to reach critical mass on willingness to fully accept LGBT people in leadership. It's been a long, hard struggle. I've been silent on this issue for too long. It's wrong for us to have been ignoring the gifts of LGBT people. I look forward to what it will do for the church when we have full rights for gay people, including ordination. Evangelical Lutheran Minister

> Licensing and ordination is the last battle that should be fought in the church. We need to gain a broader acceptance of gay

people and a greater hospitality to them. When we've achieved that goal, then would be the time to work for ordination. The energy going into that battle right now, in my opinion, is hurting us as a denomination. Presbyterian Minister

I just came off the cabinet in my Conference. I spent the last six years as a district superintendent. Almost all of us on the cabinet agree that homosexual people should be ordained, and our bishop agrees with that position in private. Right now, though, we don't see how the church would survive that kind of change in policy. We would lose too many conservative members, and we would lose too much money. In this denomination, right now, that's what the real issue is. United Methodist Minister

The whole situation depresses me beyond words. We know that there are many priests who are gay, some celibate and some not. But those seeking to enter the priesthood who are open about their orientation face far greater barriers, even if they make clear their commitment to celibacy. This needs to change, but I have no hope of that happening anytime soon, certainly not with our current Pope. Roman Catholic Priest

The Need for LGBT People in Congregations

We increasingly recognize the need to help clergy who are warmly inclined on LGBT issues develop **the strategies *and* the courage** to take proactive steps to change attitudes within their congregations and communities. In a previous study, we had found that 64% of the clergy in mainline and evangelical Protestant congregations believed that the protection of the rights of LGBT persons is a matter of religious concern, but only 7% of those clergy have expressed that conviction in any congregational or community setting.

As shared elsewhere in this report, mainline and evangelical clergy are very much aware of what they see as the danger of losing conservatives if they are too progressive on LGBT issues. Most of them have not thought a great deal about what they are losing by *not* being more progressive! There is a tremendous need to help clergy and other religious leaders become more aware of the cost of homophobia and of not being more courageous on these issues.

Some increased awareness of the way in which homophobia has negatively impacted the image of the church has recently come from an unlikely source. David Kinnaman and Gabe Lyons of the Barna Research Group have written a book titled *Unchristian: What a New Generations Really Thinks about Christianity. . . And Why It Matters* (Baker Books, Grand Rapids, Michigan, 2007). While the Barna Research Group has done studies of many different denominations, their primarily focus has been on evangelical Christianity and their primary market has been relatively conservative.

In this book, Kinnaman and Lyons are pointing out that Christianity in general and evangelical Christianity in particular have gained a negative image with people outside the church and even with people in their twenties and thirties who are inside the church. They warn that many younger people see Christianity as too judgmental, too narrow, and too antihomosexual. They warn evangelical Christians that "we have become famous for what we oppose, rather than who we are for" [p. 26].

Motivating Greater LGBT Rights Advocacy

While the book deals with much more than attitudes toward homosexuality, that is a major focus of the concern of Kinnaman and Lyons. They point out that 91% of young adults outside the church say that "antihomosexual" accurately describes present-day Christianity [pp. 92–93]. They also share the reality that the connection of homosexuality with HIV/AIDS has affected the generosity of Christians:

> Many Christians continue to be very skeptical about donating to HIV/AIDS causes, even overseas, despite Christians' generosity in some other arenas. In one poll we found that just 14 percent of born-again Christians say they would be highly motivated to help HIV/AIDS orphans overseas... They believe God is punishing these people—or that their decisions and lifestyle deserve this outcome. [p. 95]

They point out that most young adults attending church are not convinced that homosexuality is a problem in society, and "they are embarrassed by the church's treatment of gays and lesbians" [p. 101]. The book's authors urge a warmer, more charitable view of gays and lesbians. Do not, however, be fooled into thinking that these authors are new advocates for gay and lesbian concerns. Here is Kinnaman's clear statement:

> I believe homosexual behavior is a sin, but it's no different than any other sin, no different than if I sleep with someone other than my wife or even have a momentary sexual fantasy. God created sexuality so it is good, but it can be expressed in wrong ways. [p. 108]

The authors urge less hostility toward homosexual people and the recognition that this hostility has contributed to a negative image of the church. This view coming from a relatively conservative evangelical source may have some positive impact on the kinds of rhetoric about homosexuality that one hears from conservatives. The opposition to homosexual behavior from these authors is nevertheless quite clear.

In 2001 Christian Community conducted a study of differences in perspective on several issues between young adults (19 to 35 years of age) and older adults (36 and older) who are active in congregations. This was a study involving 610 mainline Protestant congregations and resulted in the following findings related to LGBT concerns:

- Young adults are almost three times as likely as older adults (81% versus 28%) to feel that homosexuality is not a sin and to feel that homosexuality is not something that people "choose" but rather that some people simply "are" homosexual.

- 93% of young adults felt that talking about sexual issues and concerns is a good and appropriate thing to do in church settings; only 39% of older adults agreed with that view.

In that study, 87% of the young adults who are church-active said that they withheld their beliefs and opinions a significant amount of the time because they knew older members would disapprove of their views, especially regarding sexuality.

There is no question that there are some significant differences in views of homosexuality between young adults and older adults who are active in the life of congregations. Secular studies have shown that such differences also exist within the broader society. The book by Kinnaman and Lyons provides an evangelical confirmation of this same reality.

Almost all mainline Protestant denominations and many evangelical Protestant denominations are deeply concerned about the lower numbers of young adults who have participated over the past twenty years and about the "graying of congregations" as the average age in many local churches has grown year by year. Obviously many factors contribute to this reality, but certainly differences in perspective between young adults and older adults on issues like homosexuality is one of the factors.

Obviously LGBT people are far more likely to attend worship, participate in other activities, and in time become members of congregations that are welcoming and affirming of them. Estimates on the percentage of LGBT persons in North America range from 3% to 8%. Even at the lowest end of the range, the numbers involved are very significant. Churches who welcome and affirm

Motivating Greater LGBT Rights Advocacy

LGBT people can expect to see growth in other categories as well:

- Those who are family members of LGBT people and want to be a part of a faith community in which their loved ones are fully accepted.

- Those who are young adults and have a more accepting view of LGBT people. Such young adults will be far more open to invitations to participate in a welcoming and accepting church.

- Those of any age who are accepting of LGBT people and who want to be in a faith community that is accepting of them.

Since the United Church of Christ went on record as being fully accepting of LGBT people, there certainly have been some congregations that have reacted negatively and even withdrawn from the denomination. What has not gained so much attention is the reality that many United Church of Christ congregations that embrace the denomination's broad hospitality are experiencing growth, not just from those who are LGBT but also from those who are attracted to the warmer, more inclusive environment.

In the process of doing the research on which this report is based, Christian Community in fact encountered congregations of many different denominational traditions that practiced a broad, biblical hospitality and that are growing as a result. In a society in which people experience rejection and judgment in many different settings, people are hungry for the kind of full and healthy acceptance that such congregations have to offer.

The media have fed on stories of churches that withdrew from denominations because of more accepting positions on LGBT issues. People who are working against LGBT acceptance in some denominations work to create the impression that welcoming and affirming churches are likely to lose members. Making meaningful comparisons between congregations, however, is very difficult because of the large number of variables that contribute to church growth and decline. Those who want to argue against LGBT acceptance can select examples to confirm their position, but the

Silent and Undecided Friends

overall direction of what is happening in congregations in North America does not support their position.

Christian Community's research over the last decade affirms that churches with a broad hospitality, including full acceptance of LGBT persons, are very likely to grow if they do the other things that make for church growth. These growing churches are characterized by:

- A broad, biblical hospitality that is extended to all people, regardless of race, economic level, physical ability, or sexual orientation.

- A membership that is comfortable reaching out to persons who are not in the church and inviting them to participate in worship and other congregational activities.

- Careful follow-up on visitors to worship and other activities so that people know they are valued and wanted in the life of the church.

- Clearly articulated beliefs and values, accompanied by an openness to those who disagree.

- A genuine openness to new people with a willingness to include those who are new in positions of leadership and in the social networks of the congregation.

With or without LGBT acceptance, churches that do not reach out to nonmembers, do not provide a warm welcome to guests, and do not positively assimilate new people are not likely to grow. Churches that do those things and that reflect a broad, biblical hospitality are in an excellent position for growth. For a more thorough discussion on this, see the new Christian Community book: *Deep and Wide: Hospitality and the Faithful Church.*

Clergy who have been silent friends and clergy who remain undecided on LGBT issues are often almost painfully aware of the risks they take if they become openly supportive. Here are some of the costs of not being more supportive:

Motivating Greater LGBT Rights Advocacy

- The loss of involvement of LGBT persons, who are more numerous in society than most people realize.

- The cost to families who have LGBT persons and feel unable to talk about that or to feel supported by the congregation.

- The loss of involvement of young adults who have a different view of these issues than many older adults. With our churches so often in desperate need of more young adults, this is a serious matter.

- The perpetuation of a negative view of Christianity within the broader society.

- The loss of involvement of heterosexual people who find judgmental attitudes toward LGBT people unacceptable.

- The loss of gifted LGBT clergy and other professional staff like music directors and business administrators who have much to offer the church.

- The loss of the gifts of LGBT lay persons who have much to offer the church.

- The feeling of LGBT people in the church that they must keep their orientation hidden.

- The cost to youth who are themselves LGBT or who are struggling over questions of orientation. Our congregational silence may well contribute to the increased suicide risk for religious LGBT teens.

- Inadequate sexuality education for children, teens, and adults because we are not willing to discuss issues of sexuality. This reality may contribute to higher rates of HIV and other sexually transmitted diseases, more unwanted pregnancies, and less satisfactory sexual relationships in marriages.

- A failure to show the kind of expansive hospitality that God expects.

Silent and Undecided Friends

- A failure to stand firmly for human rights and justice on this and other issues.

- The insights that we can gain from those who have been oppressed and the painful reality that, by our silence, we become part of the oppression.

- The personal distress and even damage to the soul caused by the disconnect some silent friends have between their personal convictions and their public vocalization.

For a fuller discussion of the gifts that LGBT involvement brings to congregations, see our booklet *Taking a New Look: Why Congregations Need LGBT Members*.

Our conversations with people in focus groups, the survey responses, the telephone interviews, and the work with pilot congregations leave us convinced that we are at a time of great opportunity for progress on LGBT acceptance in congregations, for more progressive policies in denominations, and for more religious people to become advocates for justice toward LGBT people in society.

This can only happen, however, with increased activism on the part of all those concerned about LGBT acceptance and rights. If you are reading this report, you have a role to play in this important work. It only takes one person with a commitment to acceptance and justice to start turning around an entire congregation. Growing numbers of open and accepting congregations will change the environment at the denominational level. And Christians who are committed to justice for all people can change the laws of our country and the environment of our society. We should all prayerfully consider what our Lord is calling us to do.

Definitions

The definitions which follow are taken from *A Time to Seek* by Debra Haffner and Tim Palmer and are used by permission. Some of these terms are often thought of as "binary," defined by only two categories such as *male–female* or *gay–straight*. Many scientists think it is more appropriate to consider a range of possibilities rather than the rigid categories to which many of us are accustomed.

Sex. The biological characteristics that define human beings as male or female or intersex. **Biological sex** refers to physical characteristics such as external genitals, sex chromosomes, sex hormones and internal reproductive systems. **Natal sex** is the sex assigned at birth, which is typically based on the appearance of the external genitals. In cases where the genitals appear ambiguous, the chromosomes and hormones are then assessed to make the most appropriate sex assignment. Words that describe sex are female, male, and intersex. "Sex" is often, and inaccurately, used as a synonym for sexual intercourse.

Female	Intersex	Male

Intersexual. An individual who has atypical development of physical sex attributes, including (but not limited to) external genitals that are not easily classified as male or female, incomplete development of internal reproductive organs, variations of the sex chromosomes, overproduction or underproduction of sex-related hormones, and variant development of the testes or ovaries. Some intersex characteristics are recognized at birth; others do not become apparent until puberty or later. Intersexuals were previously known as hermaphrodites. Some individuals now prefer the term **DSD** (disorders of sexual development) to refer to intersex conditions.

Sexuality. The sexual knowledge, beliefs, attitudes, values and behaviors of individuals. Its dimensions include the anatomy, physiology and biochemistry of the sexual response and reproductive systems; gender identity, sexual orientation, roles and personality; as well as thoughts, attachments, physical and emotional expressions, and relation-ships.

Sexual Identity. An individual's sense of self as a sexual being, including natal sex, gender identity, gender role, sexual orientation and sexual self-concept. Sexual identify may also refer to the language and labels people use to define themselves. **Sexual self-concept** refers to the individual's assessment of his or her sexual identity. Development of sexual identity is a critical part of adolescence.

Sexual Orientation. An individual's enduring romantic, emotional or sexual attractions toward other persons. "Heterosexual," "homosexual" and "bisexual" are examples of specific sexual orientations, although sexual orientation falls along a continuum that ranges from exclusive heterosexuality to exclusive homosexuality. Many people are attracted in varying degrees to people of the same sex and people of the other sex. It is important to note that:

- Sexual orientation refers to feelings and identity, not necessarily behavior. Individuals do not always express their sexual orientation through their sexual behaviors.
- Sexual orientation is not a choice. It is determined by a complex interaction of biological, genetic and environmental factors.

Asexuality. Little or no romantic, emotional and/or sexual attraction toward other persons. Asexuals may also be described as **nonsexual**. Asexuality is different from **celibacy**, which is a choice not to engage in sexual behaviors with another person.

Bisexuality. An enduring romantic, emotional and/or sexual attraction toward people of all sexes. A person who identifies as bisexual may live in relationships with a partner of the other sex or of the same sex. A bisexual may be more attracted to one sex than another, equally attracted to women and men, or may consider sexual orientation and gender unimportant. The intensity of a bisexual's attractions toward one sex or another may vary over time.

Heterosexuality. An enduring romantic, emotional and/or sexual attraction toward people of the other sex. The term "straight" is commonly used to refer to heterosexual people.

Homosexuality. An enduring romantic, emotional or sexual attraction toward people of the same sex. The term "gay" can refer to homosexual women or men, while the term "lesbian" refers only to homosexual women.

Heterosexual	Bisexual	Homosexual

Gender. An individual's personal, social and/or legal status as female, male or transgender. Words that describe gender include "feminine," "masculine," and "transgender." Gender is a cultural construct that reflects a society's expectations for feminine and masculine qualities and behaviors.

Gender Identity. An individual's own sense of self as a woman, man or transgender. Gender identity may or may not conform to an individual's biological sex.

Gender Expression. The outward expression (behavior, clothing, hairstyle, voice and/or body characteristics) of an individual's gender.

Gender Role. The cultural expectations of female and male behaviors.

Gender Variance. Gender identities, expressions or roles that do not conform to what society typically expects from an individual based on his or her biological sex.

Feminine　　　　　　　Gender Variant　　　　　　　Masculine

Transgender. An umbrella term for individuals whose gender identity and/or gender expression differs from the cultural expectations of their biological sex. Transgender people seek to make their gender expression match their gender identity, rather than their biological sex. The term "transgender" does not provide information about a person's sexual orientation; transgender people can be bisexual, heterosexual, homosexual or asexual.

Transsexual. A term for persons who believe that their natal sex is incompatible with their gender identity. Biological females who live as men are called female-to-male (FTM) transsexuals, transsexual men or transmen. Biological males who live as women are called male-to-female (MTF) transsexuals, transsexual women or transwomen. Transsexuals often pursue medical procedures such as hormone treatments or gender confirmation surgery (also known as sex-reassignment surgery) to make their physical attributes conform more closely to their gender identity. Transsexuals who pursue sex-reassignment surgery may refer to themselves as pre-operative ("pre-op") or post-operative ("post-op") transsexuals. Others dislike this terminology and prefer to say they are in transition.

Cross Dresser or Transvestite. An individual who regularly dresses in attire associated with the other gender, either for sexual excitement or emotional release, or in some cases, for performance art. Cross dressers can be any sexual orientation, but are primarily heterosexual men. Transvestites differ from transsexuals in that they do not want to alter their bodies. In the U.S., the older term "transvestite" is considered by many cross dressers to be offensive, but the usage and connotation vary by culture.

Silent and Undecided Friends

LGBT / GLBT. A collective acronym for lesbian, gay, bisexual and transgender people. Lengthier versions include "LGBTQ" to include people who identify as "queer," and "LGBTQQIA," to include "queer, questioning, intersex and asexual." The "a" may also be used to refer to "allies," heterosexuals who support justice for LGBT persons.

Heterosexism. Similar to racism or sexism, this term refers to the privileging of heterosexuality over other sexual orientations, or to the assumption or assertion of heterosexuality as the preferred cultural norm.

Homophobia. Fear, dislike, hatred or prejudice toward homosexuality and homosexual persons.

Queer. Once a negative term for a lesbian or gay man, "queer" has recently been reclaimed by some gay people as a self-affirming reference for anyone of a non-heterosexual orientation or gender identity. It is best not to use this word to refer to specific individuals without their consent.

Questioning. Some individuals do not identify with any of the current terms that define sexual orientation or gender identity; others are struggling to understand their own sexual orientation and/or gender identity. They may choose to refer to themselves as "questioning," "third gender", "gender queer", or they may choose no term at all.

Organizations You May Wish to Know About

The LGBT Rights Manual: Strategies for People of Faith provides a much fuller listing of organizations and of resources related to the intersection of religion and LGBT concerns. This briefer listing provides contact information for some of the organizations doing work in this area, including the welcoming and affirming organizations for several denominations.

Christian Community
6404 South Calhoun Street
Fort Wayne, IN 46807
260-456-5010
800-774-3360
www.churchstuff.com

Religious Institute for Sexual Morality, Justice, and Healing
21 Charles Street, #140
Westport, CT 06880
203-222-0055
www.religiousinstitute.org

Institute for Welcoming Resources
(Part of the National Gay and Lesbian Task Force)
810 West 31st Street Minneapolis, MN 55408
612-821-IFWR (4397)
www.welcomingresources.org/index.htm

National Gay and Lesbian Task Force
1325 Massachusetts Avenue NW, Suite 600 Washington, DC 20005 202-393-5177
www.thetaskforce.org

PFLAG (Parents, Families and Friends of Lesbians and Gays)
1726 M Street NW, Suite 400
Washington, DC 20036
202-467-8180
www.pflag.org

Silent and Undecided Friends

Progressive Christians Uniting
Suite 1104
316 W. Second Street
Los Angeles, CA 90012
213-989-1630
www.progressivechristiansuniting.org

Center for Lesbian and Gay Studies in Religion
Pacific School of Religion
1798 Scenic Avenue Berkeley, CA 94709
800-999-0528
www.clgs.org

LGBTQ Religious Studies Center
Chicago Theological Seminary
1164 E. 58th Street
Chicago, IL 60637
773-752-5757
www.ctschicago.edu/academic/lgbtq.php

Freedom to Marry
116 West 23rd Street Suite 500 New York, NY 10011
212-851-8418
www.freedomtomarry.org

Human Rights Campaign
1640 Rhode Island Avenue NW
Washington, DC 20036-3278
800-777-4723
www.hrc.org

GLAAD (Gay and Lesbian Alliance Against Defamation)
248 West 35th Street, 8th Floor New York, NY 10001
212-629-3322
www.glaad.org

GLSEN (Gay, Lesbian and Straight Education Network)
90 Broad Street, 2nd Floor New York, NY 10004
212-727-0135
www.glsen.org

National Black Justice Coalition
700 12th Street NW, Suite 700
Washington, DC 20006
202-349-3755
www.nbjcoalition.org

Soulforce, Inc.
P.O. Box 3195
Lynchburg, VA 24503-0195
www.soulforce.org

National Center for Transgender Equality
1325 Massachusetts Avenue, Suite 700
Washington, DC 20005
202-903-0112
www.nctequality.org

National Youth Advocacy Coalition
1638 R Street, NW, Suite 300
Washington, DC 20009
202-319-7596
www.nyacyouth.org/

Intersex Society of North America
979 Golf Course Drive #282
Rohnert Park, CA 94928
www.isna.org

SIECUS (Sexuality Information and Education Council of the United States)
130 West 42nd Street, Suite 350
New York, NY 10036-7802
212-819-9770
www.siecus.org

Association of Welcoming and Affirming Baptists
P.O. Box 259257
Madison, WI 53725
608-255-2155
www.wabaptists.org

Silent and Undecided Friends

Brethren Mennonite Council for Lesbian, Gay, Bisexual and Transgender Interests
P.O. Box 6300
Minneapolis, MN 55406
612-343-2060
www.bmclgbt.org/index.shtml

Coalition for LGBT Concerns
United Church of Christ
2592 West 14th Street
Cleveland, OH 44113
800-653-0799
www.ucccoalition.org

Lesbian, Gay, Bisexual and Transgender Ministries
United Church of Christ National Offices
700 Prospect Avenue
Cleveland, OH 44115
216-736-3217
www.ucc.org/lgbt/

Covenant Network of Presbyterians
2515 Fillmore Street
San Francisco, CA 94115
415-351-2196
www.covenantnetwork.org/home.htm

Dignity USA (Gay, Lesbian, Bisexual and Transgender Catholics)
P.O. Box 15373
Washington, DC 20003-5373
800-877-8797
www.dignityusa.org

Evangelicals Concerned
P.O. Box 19734
Seattle, WA 98109-6734
866-979-3297
www.ecwr.org/

Gay and Lesbian Acceptance (GALA) (Community of Christ)
P.O. Box 2173
Independence, MO 64055
www.galaweb.org

GLAD (Gay, Lesbian, Affirming Disciples) (Disciples of Christ)
P.O. Box 44400
Indianapolis, IN 46244-0400
www.gladalliance.org

Integrity (Episcopal Church USA)
620 Park Avenue, #311
Rochester, NY 14607-2943
800-462-9498
www.integrityusa.org

Kinship International (Seventh Day Adventist)
P.O. Box 69
Tillamook, OR 97141-0069
www.sdakinship.org

Lutherans Concerned / North America
P.O. Box 4707
St. Paul, MN 55104-0707
651-665-0861
www.lcna.org

More Light Presbyterians
4737 County Road 101, PMB #246
Minnetonka, MN 55345-2634
505-820-7082
www.mlp.org

Office of Bisexual, Gay, Lesbian, and Transgender Concerns
Unitarian Universalist Association
25 Beacon Street
Boston, MA 02108
617-742-2100, ext. 301
www.uua.org

Silent and Undecided Friends

Reconciling Ministries Network (United Methodist)
3801 N. Keeler Avenue
Chicago, IL 60641
773-736-5526
www.rmnetwork.org/index.html

Reconciling Pentecostals International
34522 N. Scottsdale Road D-8, Suite 238
Scottsdale, AZ 85262
480-595-6517
www.rpifellowship.com/index.html

Room for All (LGBTs in the Reformed Church in America)
26 Railroad Avenue, Box # 341
Babylon, NY 11702
www.roomforall.org

Sanctuary (Moravian Church)
P.O. Box 5053
Bethlehem, PA 18015
www.geocities.com/sanctuary_home/

Friends for Lesbian, Gay, Bisexual, Transgender, and Queer Concerns (Quaker/Friends)
www.quaker.org/flgbtqc

Universal Fellowship of Metropolitan Community Churches
P.O. Box 1374
Abilene, TX 79604
310-360-8640
www.mcchurch.org/

Affirmation (Gay & Lesbian Mormons)
P.O. Box 46022
Los Angeles, CA 90046
661-367-2421
www.affirmation.org

Jewish Mosaic:
www.jewishmosaic.org

Resources from Christian Community

Taking a New Look: Why Congregations Need LGBT Members.
This booklet offers ten focused reasons why congregations need LGBT members and endeavors to speak to some of the fears church leaders have of greater openness to LGBT people. It is designed for reading both by clergy and by lay persons in congregations. Quantity pricing is available.

Silent and Undecided Friends: Motivating Great LGBT Rights Advocacy Among Clergy and Congregations.
This is the report you are reading right now! This report gives the results of our extensive surveys and interviews with North American clergy.

LGBT Rights: A Strategy Manual for People of Faith.
This manual, being released in the spring of 2008, provides a wide range of strategies for working on greater LGBT acceptance in congregations and in other settings. The manual is based not only on the surveys and interviews referred to in this report but also on pilot work with 61 congregations.

A Time to Seek: Study Guide on Sexual and Gender Diversity by Timothy Palmer and Rev. Debra W. Haffner.
This publication provides valuable factual information that can help faith communities understand and respond to sexual and gender diversity.

Faith Matters: Teenagers, Sexuality, and Religion by Steve Clapp, Kristen Leverton Helbert, and Angela Zizak.
This book gives the results of a national study of 5,819 teens from thirty different denominations showing how their faith and congregational activity relate to their sexual values and behaviors. It includes valuable information on gay and lesbian teens.

The Gift of Sexuality: Empowerment for Religious Teens by Steve Clapp.
This book is an outgrowth of the *Faith Matters* project and is designed for use by teens in congregational settings and also for

Silent and Undecided Friends

personal reading. An *Adult Guide* is also available to accompany this resource.

Deep and Wide: Hospitality and the Faithful Church by Steve Clapp, Fred Bernhard, and Ed Bontrager. This book, designed for congregation-wide study, helps congregations look at what it means to have a hospitality that is deep and wide enough not only to bring people into membership but to thoroughly assimilate them into the life of the church. The book talks openly about the inclusion of sexual minorities as part of the church's ministry.

For information on ordering those resources, contact Christian Community at the address, phone, e-mail, or website listed below:

Christian Community
6404 South Calhoun Street
Fort Wayne, IN 46807
800-774-3360
DadofTia@aol.com
www.churchstuff.com